Francis Marion Crawford

Zoroaster

Francis Marion Crawford

Zoroaster

ISBN/EAN: 9783744726832

Printed in Europe, USA, Canada, Australia, Japan

Cover: Foto ©Andreas Hilbeck / pixelio.de

More available books at **www.hansebooks.com**

BY

F. MARION CRAWFORD

AUTHOR OF 'MR. ISAACS,' 'DR. CLAUDIUS, 'A ROMAN SINGER,'
ETC.

𝔏𝔬𝔫𝔡𝔬𝔫

MACMILLAN AND CO.

AND NEW YORK

1890

TO

My Beloved Wife

I DEDICATE THIS DRAMA

CHAPTER I.

THE hall of the banquets was made ready for the feast in the palace of Babylon. That night Belshazzar the king would drink wine with a thousand of his lords, and be merry before them; and everything was made ready.

From end to end of the mighty nave, the tables of wood, overlaid with gold and silver, stood spread with those things which the heart of man can desire; with cups of gold and of glass and of jade; with great dishes heaped high with rare fruits and rarer flowers; and over all, the last purple rays of the great southern sun came floating through the open colonnades of the porch, glancing on the polished marbles, tinging with a softer hue the smooth red plaster of the walls, and lingering lovingly on the golden features and the red-gold draperies of the vast statue that sat on high and overlooked the scene.

On his head the head-dress of thrice royal supremacy, in his right hand and his left the sceptre of power and the winged wheel of immortality and life, beneath his feet the bowed necks of prostrate captives; —so sat the kingly presence of great Nebuchadnezzar, as waiting to see what should come to pass upon his son; and the perfume of the flowers and the fruits and the rich wine came up to his mighty nostrils, and he seemed to smile there in the evening sunlight, half in satisfaction, half in scorn.

On each side of the great building, in the aisles and wings, among the polished pillars of marble thronged the serving-men, bearing ever fresh spices and flowers and fruits, wherewith to deck the feast, whispering together in a dozen Indian, Persian and Egyptian dialects, or in the rich speech of those nobler captives whose pale faces and eagle eyes stood forth everywhere in strong contrast with the coarser features and duskier skins of their fellows in servitude, —the race not born to dominate, but born to endure even to the end. These all mingled together in the strange and broken reflections of the evening light, and here and there the purple dye of the sun tinged the white tunic of some poor slave to as fair a colour as a king's son might wear.

On this side and on that of the tables that were spread for the feast, stood great candlesticks, as tall as the height of two men, tapering from the thickness and heavy carving below to the fineness and delicate tracery above, and bearing upon them cups of bronze, each having its wick steeped in fine oil mixed with wax. Moreover, in the midst of the hall, where the seat of the king was put upon a raised floor, the pillars stood apart for a space, so that there was a chamber, as it were, from the wall on the right to the wall on the left, roofed with great carved rafters; and the colour of the walls was red,—a deep and glorious red that seemed to make of the smooth plaster a sheet of precious marble. Beyond, beneath the pillars, the panels of the aisles were pictured and made many-coloured with the story of Nebuchadnezzar the king, his conquests and his feasts, his captives and his courtiers, in endless train upon the splendid wall. But where the king should sit in the midst of the hall there were neither pillars nor paintings; only the broad blaze of the royal colour, rich and even. Beside the table also stood a great lamp, taller and more cunningly wrought than the rest,—the foot of rare marble and chiselled bronze and the lamp above of pure gold from southern Ophir. But it was not yet kindled, for the sun was not set and the hour for the feast was not fully come.

At the upper end of the hall, before the gigantic statue of wrought gold, there was an open space, un-encumbered by tables, where the smooth, polished marble floor came to view in all its rich design and colour. Two persons, entering the hall with slow steps, came to this place and stood together, looking up at the face of the golden king.

Between the two there was the gulf of a lifetime. The one was already beyond the common limit of age, while he who stood beside him was but a fair boy of fourteen summers.

The old man was erect still, and his snowy hair and beard grew like a lion's mane about his massive brow and masterful face. The deep lines of thought, graven deeper by age, followed the noble shaping of his brows in even course, and his dark eyes still shot fire, as piercing the bleared thickness of time to gaze boldly on the eternity beyond. His left hand gathered the folds of a snow-white robe around him, while in his right he grasped a straight staff of ebony and ivory, of fine workmanship, marvellously polished, whereon were wrought strange sayings in the Israelitish manner of writing. The old man stood up to his noble height, and looked from the burnished face of the king's image to the eyes of the boy beside him, in silence, as though urging his young companion to speak for him the thoughts that filled the hearts of both.

The youth spoke not, nor gave any sign, but stood with folded hands and gazed up to the great features of Nebuchadnezzar.

He was but fourteen years of age, tall and delicately made, full of the promise of a graceful and elastic power, fine of skin, and instinct with the nervous strength of a noble and untainted race. His face was fair and white, tinged with faint colour, and his heavy golden hair fell in long curls upon his shoulders, thick and soft with the silken fineness of early youth. His delicate features were straight and noble, northern rather than Oriental in their type—supremely calm and thoughtful, almost god-like in their young restfulness. The deep blue eyes were turned upward with a touch of sadness, but the broad forehead was as marble, and the straight marking of the brows bounded it and divided it from the face. He wore the straight white tunic, edged about with fine embroideries of gold and gathered at the waist with a rich belt, while his legs were covered with wide Persian trousers wrought in many colours of silk upon fine linen. He wore also a small cap of linen, stiffened to a point and worked with a cunning design in gold and silver. But the old man's head was covered only by the thick masses of his snowy hair, and his wide white mantle hid the details of his dress from view.

Again he glanced from the statue to his companion's eyes, and at last he spoke, in a deep smooth voice, in the Hebrew tongue.

"Nebuchadnezzar the king is gathered to his fathers, and his son also, and Nabonnedon Belshazzar reigns in his stead, yet have I endured to this day, in Babylon, these threescore and seven years, since Nebuchadnezzar the king destroyed our place upon the earth and led us away captive. Unto this day, Zoroaster, have I endured, and yet a little longer shall I stand and bear witness for Israel."

The old man's eyes flashed, and his strong aquiline features assumed an expression of intense vitality and life. Zoroaster turned to him and spoke softly, almost sadly :

"Say, O Daniel, prophet and priest of the Lord, why does the golden image seem to smile to-day? Are the times accomplished of thy vision which thou sawest in Shushan, in the palace, and is the dead king glad? I think his face was never so gentle before to look upon,—surely he rejoices at the feast, and the countenance of his image is gladdened."

"Nay, rather then should his face be sorrowful for the destruction of his seed and of his kingdom," answered the prophet somewhat scornfully. "Verily the end is at hand, and the stones of Babylon shall no longer cry out for the burden of the sins of Belshazzar, and the people call upon Bel to restore unto life the King Nebuchadnezzar ; nay, or to send hither a Persian or a Mede to be a just ruler in the land."

"Hast thou read it in the stars, or have thine eyes seen these things in the visions of the night, my master?" The boy came nearer to the aged prophet and spoke in low earnest tones. But Daniel only bent his head, till his brow touched his ebony staff, and so he remained, deep in thought.

"For I also have dreamed,"—continued Zoroaster, after a short pause,—" and my dream took hold of me, and I am sorry and full of great weariness. Now this is the manner of my dreaming." He stopped and glanced down the great nave of the hall through the open porch at the other end. The full glory of the red sun, just touching the western plain, streamed upon his face and made the tables, the preparations and the crowd of busy serving-men look like black shadows between him and the light. But Daniel leaned upon his staff and spoke no word, nor moved from his position.

" I saw in my dream," said Zoroaster, "and there was darkness ; and upon the winds of the night arose the sound of war, and the cry and the clash of battle, mighty men striving one with another for the mastery and the victory, which should be to the stronger. And I saw again, and behold it was morning, and the people were led away captive, by tens, and by hundreds, and by thousands, and the maidens also and young women into a far country. And I looked, and the face of one of the maidens was as the face of the fairest among the daughters of thy people. Then my heart yearned for her, and I would have followed after into the captivity; but darkness came upon me, and I saw her no more. Therefore am I troubled and go heavily all the day."

He ceased and the cadence of the boy's voice trembled and was sad. The sun set out of sight beneath the plain, and from far off a great sound of music came in upon the evening breeze.

Daniel raised his snowy head and gazed keenly on his young companion, and there was disappointment in his look.

" Wouldst thou be a prophet ?" he asked, " thou that dreamest of fair maidens and art disquieted for the love of a woman ? Thinkest thou, boy, that a woman shall

help thee when thou art grown to be a man, or that
the word of the Lord dwelleth in vanity? Prophesy,
and interpret thy vision, if so be that thou art able to
interpret it. Come, let us depart, for the king is at
hand, and the night shall be given over for a space to
the rioters and the mirth-makers, with whom our portion is not. Verily I also have dreamed a dream.
Let us depart."

The venerable prophet stood up to his height, and
grasping his staff in his right hand, began to lead the
way from the hall. Zoroaster laid hold of him by the
arm, as though entreating him to remain.

"Speak, master," he cried earnestly, "and declare to
me thy dream, and see whether it accords with mine,
and whether there shall be darkness and rumour of
war in the land."

But Daniel the prophet would not stay to speak,
but went out of the hall, and Zoroaster the Persian
youth went with him, pondering deeply on the present
and on the future, and on the nature of the vision he
had seen; and made fearful by the silence of his friend
and teacher.

The darkness fell upon the twilight, and within the
hall the lamps and candlesticks were kindled and gave
out warm light and rare perfumes. All down the endless rows of tables, the preparations for the feast were
ready; and from the gardens without, strains of music
came up ever stronger and nearer, so that the winged
sounds seemed to come into the vast building and
hover above the tables and seats of honour, preparing
the way for the guests. Nearer and nearer came
the harps and the pipes and the trumpets and the
heavy reed-toned bagpipes, and above all the strong
rich chorus of the singers chanting high the evening

hymn of praise to Bel, god of sunlight, honoured in his
departing, as in his coming, with the music of the
youngest and most tuneful voices in Shinar.

First came the priests of Bel, two and two, robed
in their white tunics, loose white garments on their
legs, the white mitre of the priestly order on their
heads, and their great beards curled smooth and glossy
as silk.   In their midst, with stately dignity, walked
their chief, his eyes upon the ground, his hands crossed
upon his breast, his face like dark marble in the twilight.   On either side, those who had officiated at the
sacrifice, bore the implements of their service,—the
knife, the axe, the cord, and the fire in its dish; and
their hands were red with the blood of the victim
lately slain.   Grand, great men, mighty of body and
broad of brow, were these priests of Bel,—strong with
the meat and the wine of the offerings that were their
daily portion, and confident in the faith of their ancient
wisdom.

After the priests the musicians, one hundred chosen
men of skill, making strange deep harmonies in a noble
and measured rhythm, marching ten and ten abreast, in
ten ranks; and as they came on, the light streaming
from the porch of the palace caught their silver ornaments and the strange shapes of their instruments in
broken reflections between the twilight and the glare
of the lamps.

Behind these came the singers,—of young boys two
hundred, of youths a hundred, and of bearded men also
a hundred; the most famous of all that sang praises
to Bel in the land of Assur.   Ten and ten they marched,
with ordered ranks and step in time to the massive beat
of the long-drawn measure.

" *Mighty to rule the day, great in his glory and the*
  pride of his heat,
Shooting great bolts of light into the dark earth,
  turning death into life,
Making the seed to grow, strongly and fairly, high
  in furrow and field,
Making the heart of man glad with his gladness,
  rideth over the dawn
    Bel, the prince, the king of kings.

" *Hotly his flaming hair, streaming with brightness,*
  and the locks of his beard
Curl'd into clouds of heat, sweeping the heavens,
  spread all over the sky :
Who shall abide his face, fearful and deadly, when
  he devours the land,
Angry with man and beast, horribly raging, hungry
  for sacrifice ?
    Bel, the prince, the king of kings.

" *Striding his three great strides, out of the morning*
  through the noon to the night,
Cometh he down at last, ready for feasting, ready
  for sacrifice :
Then doth he tread the wine, purple and golden,
  foaming deep in the west ;
Shinar is spread for him, spread as a table, Assur
  shall be his seat :
    Bel, the prince, the king of kings.

" *Bring him the fresh-slain flesh, roast it with fire,*
  with the savour of salt,
Pour him the strength of wine, chalice and goblet,
  trodden for him alone :

Raise him the song of songs, cry out in praises, cry out and supplicate
That he may drink delight, tasting our off'ring, hearing our evening song:
  . Bel, the prince, the king of kings.

" So, in the gentle night, when he is resting, peace descendeth on earth;
High in the firmament, where his steps led him, gleam the tracks of his way:
Where the day felt his touch, there the night also breaketh forth into stars,
These are the flowers of heaven, garlands of blossoms, growing to weave his crown:
      Bel, the prince, the king of kings.

" Hail! thou king of the earth, hail! Belteshazzar, hail! and for ever live!
Born of the gods on high, prince of the nations, ruling over the world:
Thou art the son of Bel, full of his glory, king over death and life;
Let all the people bow, tremble and worship, bow them down and adore
      The prince of Bel, the king of kings."

As the musicians played and the singers sang, they divided their ranks and came and stood on each side of the broad marble staircase; and the priests had done so before them, but the chief priest stood alone on the lowest step.

Then, between the files of those who stood, advanced the royal procession, like a river of gold and purple and precious stones flowing between banks of pure white. Ten and ten, a thousand lords of Babylon marched in stately throng, and in their midst rode Belshazzar the king, high upon his coal-black steed, crowned with the great tiara of white linen and gold and jewels, the golden sceptre of the kingdom in his right hand. And after the lords and the king came a long procession of litters borne by stalwart slaves, wherein reclined the fairest women of all Assyria, bidden to the great feast. Last of all, the spearmen of the guard in armour all chased with gold, their mantles embroidered with the royal cognisance, and their beards trimmed and curled in the close soldier fashion, brought up the rear; a goodly company of men of war.

As the rich voices of the singers intoned the grand plain chant of the last stanza in the hymn, the king was in the middle of the open space at the foot of the staircase; there he drew rein and sat motionless on his horse, awaiting the end. As the ripe corn bends in its furrows to the wind, so the royal host around turned to the monarch, and fell upon their faces as the music died away at the signal of the high priest. With one consent the lords, the priests, the singers and the spearmen bowed and prostrated themselves on the ground; the bearers of the litters set down their burden while they did homage; and each of those beautiful women bent far forward, kneeling in her litter, and hid her head beneath her veil.

Only the king sat erect and motionless upon his steed, in the midst of the adoring throng. The light from the palace played strangely on his face, making the sneering smile more scornful upon his pale lips, and shading his sunken eyes with a darker shadow.

While you might count a score there was silence,

and the faint evening breeze wafted the sweet smell of the roses from the gardens to the king's nostrils, as though even the earth would bring incense of adoration to acknowledge his tremendous power.

Then the host rose again and fell back on either side while the king rode to the staircase and dismounted, leading the way to the banquet; and the high priest followed him and all the ranks of the lords and princes and the ladies of Babylon, in their beauty and magnificence, went up the marble steps and under the marble porch, spreading then like a river, about the endless tables, almost to the feet of the golden image of Nebuchadnezzar. And presently, from beneath the colonnades a sound of sweet music stole out again and filled the air; the serving-men hurried hither and thither, the black slaves plied their palm-leaf fans behind each guest, and the banquet was begun.

Surely, a most glorious feast, wherein the hearts of the courtiers waxed merry, and the dark eyes of the Assyrian women shot glances sweeter than the sweetmeats of Egypt and stronger than the wine of the south to move the spirit of man. Even the dark king, wasted and hollow-eyed with too much pleasure-seeking, smiled and laughed,—sourly enough at first, it is true, but in time growing careless and merry by reason of his deep draughts. His hand trembled less weakly as the wine gave him back his lost strength, and more than once his fingers toyed playfully with the raven locks and the heavy earrings of the magnificent princess at his elbow. Some word of hers roused a thought in his whirling brain.

" Is not this day the feast of victories ?" he cried in sudden animation; and there was silence to catch the king's words. " Is not this the day wherein

my sire brought home the wealth of the Israelites,
kept holy with feasting for ever? Bring me the
vessels of the unbelievers' temple, that I may drink
and pour out wine this night to Bel, the god of
gods!"

The keeper of the treasure had anticipated the king's
desire and had caused everything to be made ready;
for scarcely had Belshazzar spoken when a long train
of serving-men entered the hall of the banquet and
came and stood before the royal presence, their white
garments and the rich vessels they bore aloft standing
vividly out against the deep even red of the opposite
wall.

"Let the vessels be distributed among us," cried
the king,—"to every man a cup or a goblet till all are
served."

And so it was done, and the royal cup-bearer came
and filled the huge chalice that the king held, and the
serving-men hastened to fill all the cups and the small
basins; while the lords and princes laughed at the
strange shapes, and eyed greedily enough the thickness
and the good workmanship of the gold and silver.
And so each man and each woman had a vessel from
the temple of Jerusalem wherein to drink to the glory
of Bel the god and of Belshazzar his prince. And
when all was ready, the king took his chalice in his
two hands and stood up, and all that company of
courtiers stood up with him, while a mighty strain of
music burst through the perfumed air, and the serving-
men showered flowers and sprinkled sweet odours on
the tables.

Without stood the Angel of Death, whetting his
sword upon the stones of Babylon. But Belshazzar
held the chalice and spoke with a loud voice to the

princes and the lords and the fair women that stood about the tables in the great hall:

"I, Belshazzar the king, standing in the hall of my fathers, do pour and drink this wine to the mighty majesty of Bel the great god, who lives for ever and ever; before whom the gods of the north and of the west and of the east and of the south are as the sand of the desert in the blast; at whose sight the vain deities of Egypt crumbled into pieces, and the God of the Israelites trembled and was made little in the days of Nebuchadnezzar my sire. And I command you, lords and princes of Babylon, you and your wives and your fair women, that ye also do pour wine and drink it, doing this homage to Bel our god, and to me, Belshazzar the king."

And so saying, he turned about to one side and spilled a few drops of wine upon the marble floor, and set the cup to his lips, facing the great throng of his guests; and he drank. But from all the banquet went up a great shout.

"Hail! king, live for ever! Hail! prince of Bel, live for ever! Hail! king of kings, live for ever!" Long and loud was the cry, ringing and surging through the pillars and up to the great carved rafters till the very walls seemed to rock and tremble with the din of the king's praise.

Slowly Belshazzar drained the cup to the dregs, while with half-closed eyes he listened to the uproar, and perhaps sneered to himself behind the chalice, as was his wont. Then he set the vessel down and looked up. But as he looked he staggered and turned pale, and would have fallen; he grasped the ivory chair behind him and stood trembling in every joint, and his knees knocking together, while his eyes seemed starting from his head, and all his face was changed and distorted with dreadful fear.

Upon the red plaster of the wall, over against the candlestick which shed its strong rays upon the fearful sight, the fingers of a vast hand moved and traced letters. Only the fingers could be seen, colossal and of dazzling brightness, and as they slowly did their work, huge characters of fire blazed out upon the dark red surface, and their lambent angry flame dazzled those who beheld, and the terror of terrors fell upon all the great throng; for they stood before Him whose shadow is immortality and death.

In a silence that could be felt, the dread hand completed its message and vanished out of sight, but the strange fire burned bright in the horrid characters of the writing that remained upon the wall.

This was the inscription in Chaldean letters:

SUTMM
IPKNN
NRLAA

Then at last the king found speech and shrieked aloud wildly, and he commanded that they should bring in all the astrologers, the Chaldeans and the diviners, for he was in great terror and he dreaded some fearful and imminent catastrophe.

"Whoever shall read this writing," he cried, his voice changed and broken, "and declare to me the meaning of it, shall be clothed in purple, and shall have a chain of gold about his neck and shall rule as the third in the kingdom."

Amidst the mighty confusion of fear, the wise men were brought in before the king.

CHAPTER II.

In Ecbatana of Media Daniel dwelt in his extreme old age. There he built himself a tower within the seven-fold walls of the royal fortress, upon the summit of the hill, looking northward towards the forests of the mountains, and southward over the plain, and eastward to the river, and westward to Mount Zagros. His life was spent, and he was well-nigh a hundred years old. Seventeen years had passed since he had interpreted the fatal writing on the wall of the banquet-hall in Babylon in the night when Nabonnedon Belshazzar was slain, and the kingdom of the Assyrians destroyed for ever. Again and again invested with power and with the governorship of provinces, he had toiled un-ceasingly in the reigns of Cyrus and Cambyses, and though he was on the very boundary of possible life-time, his brain was unclouded, and his eye keen and undimmed still. Only his grand figure was more bent and his step slower than before.

He dwelt in Ecbatana of the north, in the tower he had built for himself.[1] In the midst of the royal palaces of the stronghold he had laid the foundations duly to the north and south, and story upon story had risen, row upon row of columns, balcony upon balcony of black marble, sculptured richly from basement to

---

[1] Josephus, *Antiquities of the Jews*, book x. chap. xi. 7.

turret, and so smooth and hard, that its polished corners and sides and ornaments glittered like black diamonds in the hot sun of the noonday, and cast back the moonbeams at night in a darkly brilliant reflection.

Far down below, in the gorgeous dwellings that filled the interior of the fortress, dwelt the kinsfolk of the aged prophet, and the families of the two Levites who had remained with Daniel and had chosen to follow him to his new home in Media rather than to return to Jerusalem under Zerubbabel, when Cyrus issued the writ for the rebuilding of the temple. There lived also in the palace Zoroaster, the Persian prince, being now in the thirty-first year of his age, and captain of the city and of the stronghold. And there, too, surrounded by her handmaidens and slaves, in a wing of the palace apart from the rest, and more beautiful for its gardens and marvellous adornment, lived Nehushta, the last of the descendants of Jehoiakim the king remaining in Media; she was the fairest of all the women in Media, of royal blood and of more than royal beauty.

She was born in that year when Babylon was overthrown, and Daniel had brought her with him to Shushan when he had quitted Assyria, and thence to Ecbatana. In the care of the prophet's kinswomen the little maid had thrived and grown fair in the stranger's land. Her soft child's eyes had lost their wondering look and had turned very proud and dark, and the long black lashes that fringed the heavy lids drooped to her cheek when she looked down. Her features were noble and almost straight in outline, but in the slight bend at the beginning of the nose, in the wide curved nostrils, the strong full lips, and in the pale olive skin, where the blood ebbed and flowed so generously, the signs of the Jewish race were all present and unmistakable.

Nehushta, the high-born lady of Judah, was a princess in every movement, in every action, in every word she uttered. The turn of her proud head was sovereign in its expression of approval or contempt, and Zoroaster himself bowed to the simple gesture of her hand as obediently as he would have done before the Great King in all his glory. Even the venerable prophet, sitting in his lofty tower high above the city and the fortress, absorbed in the contemplation of that other life which was so very near to him, smiled tenderly and stretched out his old hands to greet Nehushta when she mounted to his chamber at sunset, attended by her maidens and her slaves. She was the youngest of all his kinsfolk— fatherless and motherless, the last direct descendant of King Jehoiakim remaining in Media, and the aged prophet and governor cherished her and loved her for her royalty, as well as for her beauty and her kinship to himself. Assyrian in his education, Persian in his adherence to the conquering dynasty and in his long and faithful service of the Persians, Daniel was yet in his heart, as in his belief, a true son of Judah; proud of his race and tender of its young branches, as though he were himself the father of his country and the king of his people.

The last red glow of the departed day faded and sank above the black Zagros mountains to westward. The opposite sky was cold and gray, and all the green plain turned to a dull soft hue as the twilight crept over it, ever darker and more misty. In the gardens of the palace the birds in thousands sang together in chorus, as only Eastern birds do sing at sunrise and at nightfall, and their voices sounded like one strong, sweet, high chord, unbroken and drawn out.

Nehushta wandered in the broad paths alone.   The dry warm air of the summer's evening had no chill in it, and though a fine woven mantle of purple from Srinagur hung loosely from her shoulders, she needed not to draw it about her.   The delicate folds of her upper tunic fell closely around her to her knees, and were gathered at the waist by a magnificent belt of wrought gold and pearls; the long sleeves, drawn in at the wrist by clasps of pearls, almost covered her slender hands; and as she walked her delicate feet moved daintily in rich embroidered sandals with high golden heels, below the folds of the wide trousers of white and gold embroidery, gathered in at the ankle. Upon her head the stiff linen tiara of spotless white sat proudly as a royal crown, the folds of it held by a single pearl of price, and from beneath it her magnificent hair rolled down below her waist in dark smooth waves.

There was a terrace that looked eastward from the gardens.   Thither Nehushta bent her steps, slowly, as though in deep thought, and when she reached the smooth marble balustrade, she leaned over it and let her dark eyes rest on the quiet landscape.   The peace of the evening descended upon her; the birds of the day ceased singing with the growing darkness; and slowly, out of the plain, the yellow moon soared up and touched the river and the meadows with mystic light; while far off, in the rose-thickets of the gardens, the first notes of a single nightingale floated upon the scented breeze, swelling and trilling, quivering and falling again, in a glory of angelic song.   The faint air fanned her cheek, the odours of the box and the myrtle and the roses intoxicated her senses, and as the splendid shield of the rising moon cast its broad light into

her dreaming eyes, her heart overflowed, and Nehushta
the princess lifted up her voice and sang an ancient
song of love, in the tongue of her people, to a soft
minor melody, that sounded like a sigh from the
southern desert.

> " *Come unto me, my beloved, in the warmth of the*
> *darkness, come—*
> *Rise, and hasten thy footsteps, to be with me at*
> *night-time, come!*

> " *I wait in the darkness for him, and the sand of*
> *the desert whirling*
> *Is blown at the door of my tent which is open*
> *toward the desert.*

> " *My ear in the darkness listeth for the sound of his*
> *coming nearer,*
> *Mine eyes watch for him and rest not, for I would*
> *not he found me sleeping.*

> " *For when my beloved cometh, he is like the beam of*
> *the morning;* [1]
> *Ev'n as the dawn in a strange land to the sight of*
> *a man journeying.*

> " *Yea, when my beloved cometh, as dew that descend-*
> *eth from heaven,*
> *No man can hear when it falleth, but as rain it*
> *refresheth all things.*

> " *In his hand bringeth he lilies, in his right hand*
> *are many flowers,*

---

[1] "Thou art to me as the beam of the east rising in a strange land."
—*Ossian.*

*Roses hath he on his forehead, he is crowned with
    roses from Shinar.*

" *The night-winds make sweet songs for him, even in
        the darkness soft music;
Whithersoever he goeth, there his sweetness goeth
    before him.*"

Her young voice died away in a soft murmuring
cadence, and the nightingale alone poured out her
heartful of love to the ancient moon. But as Nehushta
rested immovable by the marble balustrade of the terrace, there was a rustle among the myrtles and a quick
step on the pavement. The dark maiden started at
the sound, and a happy smile parted her lips. But
she did not turn to look; only her hand stole out
behind her on the marble where she knew her lover's
would meet it. There was in the movement all the
certainty of conquest and yet all the tenderness of
love. The Persian trod quickly and laid his hand on
hers, and bent to her, trying to meet her eyes: for
one moment still she gazed out straight before her,
then turned and faced him suddenly, as though she
had withheld her welcome as long as she could and
then given it all at once.

"I did not call you," she said, covering him with
her eyes in the moonlight, but making as though she
would withdraw herself a little from him, as he drew
her with his hand, and with his arm, and with his
eyes.

"And yet I heard you call me, my beloved," answered Zoroaster. "I heard your voice singing very
sweet things in your own language—and so I came,
for you did call me."

"But did you pride yourself it was for you?" laughed Nehushta. "I sang of the desert, and of tents, and of whirling sand—there is none of these things here."

"You said that your beloved brought roses in his hand—and so I do. I will crown you with them. May I? No—I shall spoil your head-dress. Take them and do as you will with them."

"I will take them—and—I always do as I will."

"Then will to take the giver also," answered Zoroaster, letting his arm steal about her, as he half sat upon the balustrade. Nehushta looked at him again, for he was good to see, and perhaps she loved his straight calm features the better in that his face was fair, and not dark like hers.

"Methinks I have taken the giver already," she answered.

"Not yet—not all," said Zoroaster in a low voice, and a shadow of sadness crossed his noble face that looked white in the moonlight. Nehushta sighed softly and presently she laid her cheek upon his shoulder where the folding of his purple mantle made a pillow between her face and the polished golden scales of his breastplate.

"I have strange news to tell you, beloved," said Zoroaster presently. Nehushta started and looked up, for his voice was sad. "Nay, fear not!" he continued, "there is no harm in it, I trust; but there are great changes in the kingdom, and there will be greater changes yet. The seven princes have slain Smerdis in Shushan, and Darius is chosen king, the son of Gushtasp, whom the Greeks call Hystaspes."

"He who came hither last year?" asked Nehushta quickly. "He is not fair, this new king."

"Not fair," replied the Persian, "but a brave man and a good. He has, moreover, sent for me to go to Shushan——"

"For you!" cried Nehushta, suddenly laying her two hands on Zoroaster's shoulders and gazing into his eyes. His face was to the moonlight, while hers was in the dark, and she could see every shade of expression. He smiled. "You laugh at me!" she cried indignantly. "You mock me—you are going away and you are glad!"

She would have turned away from him, but he held her two hands.

"Not alone," he answered. "The Great King has sent an order that I shall bring to Shushan the kinsfolk of Jehoiakim, saving only Daniel, our master, for he is so old that he cannot perform the journey. The king would honour the royal seed of Judah, and to that end he sends for you, most noble and most beloved princess."

Nehushta was silent and thoughtful; her hand slipped from Zoroaster's grasp, and her eyes looked dreamily out at the river, on which the beams of the now fully-risen moon glanced, as on the scales of a silver serpent.

"Are you glad, my beloved?" asked Zoroaster. He stood with his back to the balustrade, leaning on one elbow, and his right hand played carelessly with the heavy gold tassels of his cloak. He had come up from the fortress in his armour, as he was, to bring the news to Nehushta and to Daniel; his gilded harness was on his back, half-hidden by the ample purple cloak, his sword was by his side, and on his head he wore the pointed helmet, richly inlaid with gold, bearing in front the winged wheel which the sovereigns of

the Persian empire had assumed after the conquest of
Assyria. His very tall and graceful body seemed
planned to combine the greatest possible strength with
the most surpassing activity, and in his whole presence
there breathed the consciousness of ready and elastic
power, the graceful elasticity of a steel bow always
bent, the inexpressible ease of motion and the matchless swiftness that men had when the world was young
—that wholeness of harmonious proportion which alone
makes rest graceful, and the inactivity of idleness itself
like a mode of perfect motion. As they stood there
together, the princess of Judah and the noble Persian,
they were wholly beautiful and yet wholly contrasted
—the Semite and the Aryan, the dark race of the
south, on which the hot air of the desert had breathed
for generations in the bondage of Egypt, and left its
warm sign-manual of southern sunshine,—and the
fair man of the people whose faces were already set
northwards, on whom the north breathed already
its icy fairness, and magnificent coldness of steely
strength.

"Are you glad, my beloved?" asked Zoroaster
again, looking up and laying his right hand on the
princess's arm. She had given no answer to his
question, but only gazed dreamily out over the river.

She seemed about to speak, then paused again, then
hesitated and answered his question by another.

"Zoroaster—you love me," again she paused, and,
as he passionately seized her hands and pressed his
lips to them, she said softly, turning her head away,
"What is love?"

He, too, waited one moment before he answered,
and, standing to his lordly height, took her head between his hands and pressed it to his breast; then,

with one arm around her, he stood looking eastward
and spoke:

"Listen, my beloved, and I, who love you, will tell
you what love is. In the far-off dawn of the soul-
life, in the ethereal distance of the outer firmament, in
the mist of the star-dust, our spirits were quickened
with the spirit of God, and found one another, and
met. Before earth was for us, we were one; before
time was for us, we were one—even as we shall be
one when there is no time for us any more. Then
Ahura Mazda, the all-wise God, took our two souls
from among the stars, and set them in the earth,
clothed for a time with mortal bodies. But we know
each other, that we were together from the first, although
these earthly things obscure our immortal vision, and
we see each other less clearly. Yet is our love none
the less—rather, it seems every day greater, for our
bodies can feel joy and sorrow, even as our spirits do;
so that I am able to suffer for you, in which I rejoice,
and I would that I might be chosen to lay down my
life for you, that you might know how I love you; for
often you doubt me, and sometimes you doubt yourself.
There should be no doubt in love. Love is from the
first, and will be to the end, and beyond the end; love
is so eternal, so great, so whole, that this mortal life of
ours is but as a tiny instant, a moment of pausing in
our journey from one star-world to another along the
endless paths of heavenly glory we shall tread together
—it is nothing, this worldly life of ours. Before it
shall seem long that we have loved, this earth we stand
on, these things we touch, these bodies of ours that
we think so strong and fair, will be forgotten and dis-
solved into their elements in the trackless and undis-
coverable waste of past mortality, while we ourselves

are ever young, and ever fair, and for ever living in our immortal love."

Nehushta looked up wonderingly into her lover's eyes, then let her head rest on his shoulder. The high daring of his thoughts seemed ever trying to scale heaven itself, seeking to draw her to some wondrous region of mystic beauty and strange spirit life. She was awed for a moment, then she, too, spoke in her own fashion.

"I love life," she said, "I love you because you live, not because you are a spirit chained and tied down for a time. I love this soft sweet earth, the dawn of it, and the twilight of it; I love the sun in his rising and in his setting; I love the moon in her fulness and in her waning; I love the smell of the box and of the myrtle, of the roses and of the violets; I love the glorious light of day, the splendour of heat and greenness, the song of the birds of the air and the song of the labourer in the field, the hum of the locust, and the soft buzzing of the bee; I love the brightness of gold and the richness of fine purple, the tramp of your splendid' guards and the ring of their trumpets clanging in the fresh morning, as they march through the marble courts of the palace. I love the gloom of night for its softness, the song of the nightingale in the ivory moonlight, the rustle of the breeze in the dark rose-thickets, and the odour of the sleeping flowers in my gardens; I love even the cry of the owl from the prophet's tower, and the soft thick sound of the bat's wings, as he flits past the netting of my window. I love it all, for the whole earth is rich and young and good to touch, and most sweet to live in. And I love you because you are more beautiful than other men, fairer and stronger and braver, and because you love me, and will let no other love me but yourself, if you were to die for it. Ah, my beloved, I would that I had all the sweet voices of the earth, all the tuneful tongues of the air, to tell you how I love you!"

"There is no lack of sweetness, nor of eloquence, my princess," said Zoroaster; "there is no need of any voice sweeter than yours, nor of any tongue more tuneful. You love in your way, I in mine; the two together must surely be the perfect whole. Is it not so? Nay—seal the deed once again—and again—so! 'Love is stronger than death,' says your preacher."

"'And jealousy is as cruel as the grave,' he says, too," added Nehushta, her eyes flashing fire as her lips met his. "You must never make me jealous, Zoroaster, never, never! I would be so cruel—you cannot dream how cruel I would be!"

Zoroaster laughed under his silken beard, a deep, joyous, ringing laugh that startled the moonlit stillness.

"By Nabon and Bel, there is small cause for your jealousy here," he said.

"Swear not by your false gods!" laughed Nehushta. "You know not how little it would need to rouse me."

"I will not give you that little," answered the Persian. "And as for the false gods, they are well enough for a man to swear by in these days. But I will swear by any one you command me, or by anything!"

"Swear not, or you will say again that the oath has need of sealing," replied Nehushta, drawing her mantle around her, so as to cover half her face. "Tell me, when are we to begin our journey? We have talked much and have said little, as it ever is. Shall we go at once, or are we to wait for another order? Is

Darius safe upon the throne? Who is to be chiefest at the court—one of the seven princes, I suppose, or his old father? Come, do you know anything of all these changes? Why have you never told me what was going to happen—you who are high in power and know everything?"

"Your questions flock upon me like doves to a maiden who feeds them from her hand," said Zoroaster, with a smile, "and I know not which shall be fed first. As for the king, I know that he will be great, and will hold securely the throne, for he has already the love of the people from the Western sea to the wild Eastern mountains. But it seemed as though the seven princes would have divided the empire amongst them, until this news came. I think he will more likely take one of your people for his close friend than trust to the princes. As for our journey, we must depart betimes, or the king will have gone before us from Shushan to Stakhar in the south, where they say he will build himself a royal dwelling and stay in the coming winter time. Prepare yourself for the journey, therefore, my princess, lest anything be forgotten and you should be deprived of what you need for any time."

"I am never deprived of what I need," said Nehushta, half in pride and half in jest.

"Nor I, when I am with my beloved!" answered the Persian. "And now the moon is high, and I must bear this news to our master, the prophet."

"So soon?" said Nehushta reproachfully, and she turned her head away.

"I would there were no partings, my beloved, even for the space of an hour," answered Zoroaster, tenderly drawing her to him; but she resisted a little and would not look at him.

"Farewell now—good-night, my princess—light of my soul;" he kissed her dark cheek passionately. "Good-night!"

He trod swiftly across the terrace.

"Zoroaster! prince!" Nehushta called aloud, but without turning. He came back. She threw her arms about his neck and kissed him almost desperately. Then she pushed him gently away from her.

"Go—my love—only that," she murmured, and he left her standing by the marble balustrade, while the yellow moon turned slowly pale as she rose in the heavens, and the song of the lorn nightingale re-echoed in the still night, from the gardens to the towers, in long sweet cries of burning love, and soft, complaining, silvery notes of mingled sorrow and joy.

CHAPTER III.

IN the prophet's chamber, also, the moonbeams fell
upon the marble floor; but a seven-beaked Hebrew
lamp of bronze shed a warmer light around, soft and
mellow, yet strong enough to illuminate the scroll that
lay open upon the old man's knee.   His brows were
knit together, and the furrows on his face were shaded
deeply by the high light, as he sat propped among
many cushions and wrapped in his ample purple cloak
that was thickly lined with fur and drawn together
over his snowy beard; for the years of his life were
nearly accomplished, and the warmth of his body was
even then leaving him.

Zoroaster raised the heavy curtain of carpet that
hung before the low square door, and came and bowed
himself before the teacher of his youth and the friend
of his manhood.   The prophet looked up keenly, and
something like a smile crossed his stern features as his
eyes rested on the young officer in his magnificent
armour; Zoroaster held his helmet in his hand, and
his fair hair fell like a glory to his shoulders, mingling
with his silky beard upon his breastplate.   His dark
blue eyes met his master's fearlessly.

"Hail! and live for ever, chosen of the Lord!" he
said in salutation.   " I bring tidings of great moment

and importance.   If it be thy pleasure, I will speak ;
but if not, I will come at another season."

"Sit upon my right hand, Zoroaster, and tell me all
that thou hast to tell.   Art thou not my beloved son,
whom the Lord hath given me to comfort mine old
age ? "

"I am thy servant and the servant of thine house,
my father," answered Zoroaster, seating himself upon
a carved chair at a little distance from the prophet.

"Speak, my son,—what tidings hast thou ? "

"There is a messenger come in haste from Shushan,
bearing tidings and letters.   The seven princes have
slain Smerdis in his house, and have chosen Darius
the son of Gushtasp to be king."

"Praise be to the Lord who hath chosen a just
man !" exclaimed the prophet devoutly.   "So may
good come out of evil, and salvation by the shedding
of blood."

"Even so, my master," answered Zoroaster.   "It is
also written that Darius, may he live for ever, will
establish himself very surely upon the throne of the
Medes and Persians.   There are letters by the hand
of the same messenger, sealed with the signet of the
Great King, wherein I am bidden to bring the kinsfolk
of Jehoiakim, who was king over Judah, to Shushan
without delay, that the Great King may do them
honour as is meet and right ; but what that honour
may be that he would do to them, I know not."

"What is this that thou sayest ?" asked Daniel,
starting forward from his reclining position, and fixing
his dark eyes on Zoroaster.   "Will the king take
away from me the children of my old age ?   Art not
thou as my son ?   And is not Nehushta as my daughter?
As for the rest, I care not if they go.   But Nehushta

is as the apple of my eye! She is as a fair flower growing in the desert of my years! What is this that the king hath done to me? Whither will he take her from me?"

"Let not my lord be troubled," said Zoroaster, earnestly, for he was moved by the sudden grief of the prophet. "Let not my lord be troubled. It is but for a space, for a few weeks; and thy kinsfolk will be with thee again, and I also."

"A space, a few weeks! What is a space to thee, child, or a week that thou shouldest regard it? But I am old and full of years. It may be, if now thou takest my daughter Nehushta from me, that I shall see her face no more, neither thine, before I go hence and return not. Go to! Thou art young, but I am now nigh unto a hundred years old."

"Nevertheless, if it be the will of the Great King, I must accomplish this thing," answered the young man. "But I will swear by thy head and by mine that there shall no harm happen to the young princess; and if anything happen to her that is evil, may the Lord do so to me and more also. Behold, I have sworn; let not my lord be troubled any more."

But the prophet bowed his head and covered his face with his hands. Aged and childless, Zoroaster and Nehushta were to him children, and he loved them with his whole soul. Moreover, he knew the Persian Court, and he knew that if once they were taken into the whirl and eddy of its intrigue and stirring life, they would not return to Ecbatana; or returning, they would be changed and seem no more the same. He was bitterly grieved and hurt at the thought of such a separation, and in the grand simplicity of his greatness he felt no shame at shedding tears for them. Zoroaster

himself, in the pride of his brilliant youth, was overcome with pain at the thought of quitting the sage
who had been a father to him for thirty years. He
had never been separated from Daniel save for a few
months at a time during the wars of Cambyses ; at six-
and-twenty years of age he had been appointed to the
high position of captain of the fortress of Ecbatana;
since which time he had enjoyed the closest intercourse
with the prophet, his master.

Zoroaster was a soldier by force of circumstances, and
he wore his gorgeous arms with matchless grace, but there
were two things that, with him, went before his military
profession, and completely eclipsed it in importance.

From his earliest youth he had been the pupil
of Daniel, who had inspired him with his own love of
the mystic lore to which the prophet owed so much of
his singular success in the service of the Assyrian
and Persian monarchs. The boy's poetical mind,
strengthened and developed by the study of the art of
reasoning, and of the profound mathematical knowledge
of the Chaldean astronomers, easily grasped the highest
subjects, and showed from the first a capacity and
lucidity that delighted his master. To attain by a life
of rigid ascetic practice to the intuitive comprehension
of knowledge, to the understanding of natural laws not
discernible to the senses alone, and to the merging of
the soul and higher intelligence in the one universal
and divine essence, were the objects Daniel proposed
to his willing pupil. The noble boy, by his very
nature, scorned and despised the pleasures of sense,
and yearned ever for the realising of an ideal wherein
a sublime wisdom of transcendent things should direct
a sublime courage in things earthly to the doing of
great deeds.

D

Year after year the young Persian grew up in the
splendid surroundings of the court, distinguished before
all those of his age for his courage and fearless honesty,
for his marvellous beauty, and for his profound understanding of all subjects, great and small, that came
within the sphere of his activity; most of all remarkable, perhaps, for the fact that he cared nothing for
the society of women, and had never been known to
love any woman. He was a favourite with Cyrus;
and even Cambyses, steeped in degrading vice, and
surrounded by flatterers, panderers, and priests of the
Magians, from the time when he began to suspect his
brother, the real Smerdis, of designs upon the throne, recognised the exceptional merits and gifts of the young
noble, and promoted him to his position in Ecbatana, at
the time when he permitted Daniel to build his great
tower in that ancient fortress. The dissipated king
may have understood that the presence of such men
as Daniel and Zoroaster would be of greater advantage
in an outlying district where justice and moderation
would have a good effect upon the population, than in
his immediate neighbourhood, where the purity and
temperance of their lives contrasted too strongly with
the degrading spectacle his own vices afforded to the
court.

Here, in the splendid retirement of a royal palace,
the prophet had given himself up completely to the
contemplation of those subjects which, through all his
life, had engrossed his leisure time, and of which the
knowledge had so directly contributed to his singular
career; and in the many hours of leisure which Zoroaster's position allowed him, Daniel sought to bring
the intelligence of the soldier-philosopher to the perfection of its final development. Living, as he did,

entirely in his tower, save when, at rare intervals, he
caused himself to be carried down to the gardens, the
prophet knew little of what went on in the palace
below, so that he sometimes marvelled that his pupil's
attention wandered, and that his language betrayed
occasionally a keener interest in his future, and in the
possible vicissitudes of his military life, than he had
formerly been wont to show.

For a new element had entered into the current of
Zoroaster's thoughts.   For years he had seen the lovely
child Nehushta growing up.   As a boy of twenty
summers he had rocked her on his knee; later he had
taught her and played with her, and seen the little
child turn to the slender girl, haughty and royal in
her young ways, and dominating her playfellows as a
little lioness might rule a herd of tamer creatures; and
at last her sixteenth year had brought with it the
bloom of early southern womanhood, and Zoroaster,
laughing with her among the roses in the gardens, on
a summer's day, had felt his heart leap and sink within
him, and his own fair cheek grow hot and cold for the
ring of her voice and the touch of her soft hand.

He who knew so much of mankind, who had lived
so long at the court, and had coldly studied every
stage of human nature, where unbridled human nature
ever ruled the hour, knew what he felt; and it was
as though he had received a sharp wound that thrust
him through, body and heart and soul, and cleft his
cold pride in two.   For days he wandered beneath the
pines and the rhododendron trees alone, lamenting for
the fabric of mighty philosophy he had built himself,
in which no woman was ever to set foot; and which a
woman's hand, a woman's eyes had shattered in a day.
It seemed as if his whole life were blasted and de-

stroyed, so that he was become even as other men, to
suffer love and eat his heart out for a girl's fair word.
He would have escaped from meeting the dark young
princess again; but one evening, as he stood alone
upon the terrace of the gardens, sorrowing for the
change in himself, she found him, and there they
looked into each other's eyes and saw a new light, and
loved each other fiercely from that day, as only the
untainted children of godlike races could love.   But
neither of them dared to tell the prophet, nor to let
those of the palace know that they had pledged each
other their troth, down there upon the moonlit terrace,
behind the myrtles.   Instinctively they dreaded lest
the knowledge of their love should raise a storm of
anger in Daniel's breast at the idea that his chosen
philosopher should abandon the paths of mystic
learning and reduce himself to the level of common
mankind by marriage; and Zoroaster guessed how
painful to the true Israelite would be the thought that
a daughter and a princess of Judah should be united
in wedlock with one who, however noble and true and
wise, was, after all, a stranger and an unbeliever.   For
Zoroaster, while devoting himself heart and soul to the
study of Daniel's philosophy, and of the wisdom the
latter had acquired from the Chaldeans, had nevertheless firmly maintained his independence of thought.
He was not an Israelite, nor would he ever wish to
become one; but he was not an idolater nor a Magian,
nor a follower of Gomata, the half-Indian Brahmin,
who had endeavoured to pass himself off as Smerdis
the son of Cyrus.

Either of these causes alone would have sufficed to
raise a serious obstacle to the marriage.   Together
they seemed insurmountable.   During the disorder and

anarchy that prevailed in the seven months of the reign of Pseudo-Smerdis, it would have been madness to have married, trusting to the favour of the wretched semi-monarch for fortune and advancement; nor could Nehushta have married and maintained her state as a princess of Judah without the consent of Daniel, who was her guardian, and whose influence was paramount in Media, and very great even at court. Zoroaster was therefore driven to conceal his passion as best he could, trusting to the turn of future events for the accomplishment of his dearest wish. In the meanwhile, he and the princess met daily in public, and Zoroaster's position as captain of the fortress gave him numerous opportunities of meeting Nehushta in the solitude of the gardens, which were jealously guarded and set apart exclusively for the use of Nehushta and her household.

But now that the moment had come when it seemed as though a change were to take place in the destinies of the lovers, they felt constrained. Beyond a few simple questions and answers, they had not discussed the matter of the journey when they were together; for Nehushta was so much surprised and delighted at the idea of again seeing the magnificence of the court at Shushan, which she so well remembered from the period of her childhood, that she feared to let Zoroaster see how glad she was to leave Ecbatana, which, but for him, would have been to her little better than a prison. He, on the contrary, thinking that he foresaw an immediate removal of all obstacle and delay through the favour of Darius, was, nevertheless, too gentle and delicate of tact to bring suddenly before Nehushta's mind the prospect of marrying which presented itself so vividly to his own fancy. But he felt no less disturbed in his heart when face to face with the old prophet's sorrow

at losing his foster-daughter; and, for the first time in
his life, he felt guilty when he reflected that Daniel
was grieved at his own departure almost as deeply as
on account of Nehushta.   He experienced what is so
common with persons of cold and even temperament
when brought into close relation with more expansive
and affectionate natures; he was overcome with the
sense that his old master gave him more love and
more thought than he could possibly give in return,
and that he was therefore ungrateful; and the knowledge he alone possessed, that he surely intended to
marry the princess in spite of the prophet, and by
the help of the king, added painfully to his mental
suffering.

The silence lasted some minutes, till the old man
suddenly lifted his head and leaned back among his
cushions, gazing at his companion's face.

".Hast thou no sorrow, nor any regret?" he asked
sadly.

"Nay, my lord doth me injustice," answered Zoroaster, his brows contracting in his perplexity.   "I should
be ungrateful if I repented not leaving thee even for
the space of a day.   But let my lord be comforted;
this parting is not for long, and before the flocks come
down from Zagros to take shelter from the winter, we
will be with thee."

"Swear to me, then, that thou wilt return before
the winter," insisted the prophet half-scornfully.

"I cannot swear," answered Zoroaster.   "Behold, I
am in the hands of the Great King.   I cannot swear."

"Say rather that thou art in the hand of the Lord,
and that therefore thou canst not swear.   For I say
thou wilt not return, and I shall see thy face no more.
The winter cometh, and the birds of the air fly towards

the south, and I am alone in the land of snow and
frost; and the spring cometh also, and I am yet alone,
and my time is at hand; for thou comest not any
more, neither my daughter Nehushta, neither any of my
kinsfolk.   And behold, I go down to the grave alone."

The yellow light of the hanging lamp above shone
upon the old man's eyes, and there was a dull fire in
them.   His face was drawn and haggard, and every
line and furrow traced by the struggles of his hundred
years stood out dark and rugged and tremendous in
power.   Zoroaster shuddered as he looked on him, and,
though he would have spoken, he was awed to silence.

"Go forth, my son," cried the prophet in deep tones,
and as he spoke he slowly raised his body till he sat
rigidly erect, and his wan and ancient fingers were
stretched out towards the young soldier.   "Go forth
and do thy part, for thou art in the hand of the Lord,
and some things that thou wilt do shall be good, and
some things evil.   For thou hast departed from the
path of crystal that leadeth among the stars, and thou
hast fallen away from the ladder whereby the angels
ascend and descend upon the earth, and thou art gone
after the love of a woman which endureth not.   And
for a season thou shalt be led astray, and for a time
thou shalt suffer great things; and after a time thou
shalt return into the way; and again a time, and thou
shalt perish in thine own imaginations, because thou
hast not known the darkness from the light, nor the
good from the evil.   By a woman shalt thou go astray,
and from a woman shalt thou return; yet thou shalt
perish.   But because there is some good in thee, it
shall endure, and thy name also, for generations; and
though the evil that besetteth thee shall undo thee,
yet at the last thy soul shall live."

Zoroaster buried his face in his hands, overcome by the majesty of the mighty prophet and by the terror of his words.

"Rise and go forth, for the hand of the Lord is upon thee, and no man can hinder that thou doest. Thou shalt look upon the sun and shalt delight in him; and again thou shalt look and the light of the air shall be as darkness. Thou shalt boast in thy strength and in thine armour that there is none like thee, and again thou shalt cast thy glory from thee and say, 'This also is vanity.' The king delighteth in thee, and thou shalt stand before the queen in armour of gold and in fine raiment; and the end is near, for the hand of the Lord is upon thee. If the Lord will work great things by thee, what is that to me? Go forth quickly, and rest not by the way, lest the woman tempt thee and thou perish. And as for me, I go also—not with thee, but before thee. See that thou follow after—for I go. Yea, I see even now light in the darkness of the world, and the glory of the triumph of heaven is over me, triumphing greatly in the majesty of light."

Zoroaster looked up and fell to the ground upon his knees in wonder and amazement at Daniel's feet, while his heavy helmet rolled clanging on the marble pavement. The prophet stood erect as a giant oak, stretching his withered hands to heaven, all the mass of his snow-white hair and beard falling about him to his waist. His face was illuminated as from within with a strange light, and his dark eyes turned upward seemed to receive and absorb the brightness of an open heaven. His voice rang again with the strength of youth, and his whole figure was clothed as with the majesty of another world. Again he spoke:

"Behold, the voice of the ages is in me, and the
Lord my God hath taken me up. My days are
ended; I am taken up and shall no more be cast
down. The earth departeth and the glory of the Lord
is come which hath no end for ever.

"The Lord cometh—He cometh quickly. In His
right hand are the ages, and the days and the nights are
under His feet. The ranks of the Cherubim are beside
Him, and the armies of the Seraphim are dreadful.
The stars of heaven tremble, and the voice of their
moaning is as the voice of the uttermost fear. The
arch of the outer firmament is shivered like a broken
bow, and the curtain of the sky is rent in pieces as a
veil in the tempest. The sun and the moon shriek
aloud, and the sea crieth horribly before the Lord.

"The nations are extinct as the ashes of a fire that
is gone out, and the princes of the earth are no more.
He hath bruised the earth in a mortar, and the dust
of it is scattered abroad in the heavens. The stars
in their might hath He pounded to pieces, and the
foundations of the ages to fine powder. There is
nothing of them left, and their voices are dead. There
are dim shapes in the horror of emptiness.

"But out of the north ariseth a fair glory with
brightness, and the breath of the Lord breatheth life
into all things. The beam of the dawn is risen, and
there shall again be times and seasons, and the Being
of the majesty of God is made manifest in form. From
the dust of the earth is the earth made again, and of
the beams of His glory shall He make new stars.

"Send up the voices of praise, O ye things that are;
Cry out in exultation with mighty music! Praise the
Lord in whom is Life, and in whom all things have
Being! Praise Him and glorify Him that is risen

with the wings of the morning of heaven; in whose
breath the stars breathe, in whose brightness also the
firmament is lightened! Praise Him who maketh the
wheels of the spheres to run their courses; who
maketh the flowers to bloom in the spring, and the
little flowers of the field to give forth their sweetness!
Praise Him, winter and summer; praise Him, cold and
heat! Praise Him, stars of heaven; praise Him, men
and women in the earth! Praise and glory and
honour be unto the Most High Jehovah, who sitteth
upon the Throne for ever, and ever, and ever . . ."

The prophet's voice rang out with tremendous force
and majestic clearness as he uttered the last words.
Throwing up his arms to their height, he stood one
moment longer, immovable, his face radiantly illuminated with an unearthly glory. One instant he stood
there, and then fell back, straight and rigid, to his
length upon the cushioned floor—dead!

Zoroaster started to his feet in amazement and
horror, and stood staring at the body of his master and
friend lying stiff and stark beneath the yellow light of
the hanging lamp. Then suddenly he sprang forward
and kneeled again beside the pale noble head that
looked so grand in death. He took one of the hands
and chafed it, he listened for the beating of the heart
that beat no more, and sought for the stirring of the
least faint breath of lingering life. But he sought in
vain; and there, in the upper chamber of the tower,
the young warrior fell upon his face and wept alone
by the side of the mighty dead.

CHAPTER IV.

THUS died Daniel, and for seven days the women sat apart upon the ground and mourned him, while the men embalmed his body and made it ready for burial. They wrapped him in much fine linen and poured out very precious spices and ointments from the store-houses of the palaces. Round about his body they burned frankincense and myrrh and amber, and the gums of the Indian benzoe and of the Persian fir, and great candles of pure wax; for all the seven days the mourners from the city made a great mourning, ceasing not to sing the praises of the prophet and to cry aloud by day and night that the best and the worthiest and the greatest of all men was dead.

Thus they watched and mourned and sang his great deeds. And in the lower chamber of the tower the women sat upon the floor, with Nehushta in their midst, and sorrowed greatly, fasting and mourning in raiment of sackcloth, and strewing ashes upon the floor and upon themselves. Nehushta's face grew thin and very pale and her lips white in that time, and she let her heavy hair hang neglected about her. Many of the men shaved their heads and went bare-footed, and the fortress and the palaces were filled with the sound of weeping and grief. The Hebrews who were there mourned their chief, and the two

Levites sat beside the dead man and read long chapters from their scriptures. The Medes mourned their great and just governor, under the Assyrian name of Belteshazzar, given first to Daniel by Nebuchadnezzar; and from all the town the noise of their weeping and mourning came up, like the mighty groan of a nation, to the ears of those that dwelt in the fortress and the palace.

On the eighth day they buried him, with pomp and state, in a tomb in the garden which they had built during the week of mourning. The two Levites and a young Hebrew and Zoroaster himself, clad in sackcloth and barefooted, raised up the prophet's body upon a bier and bore him upon their shoulders down the broad staircase of the tower and out into the garden to his tomb. The mourners went before, many hundreds of Median women with dishevelled hair, rending their dresses of sackcloth and scattering ashes upon their path and upon their heads, crying aloud in wild voices of grief and piercing the air with their screams, till they came to the tomb and stood round about it while the four men laid their master in his great coffin of black marble beneath the pines and the rhododendrons. And the pipers followed after, making shrill and dreadful music that sounded as though some supernatural beings added their voices to the universal wail of woe. And on either side of the body walked the women, the prophet's kinsfolk; but Nehushta walked by Zoroaster, and ever and anon, as the funeral procession wound through the myrtle walks of the deep gardens, her dark and heavy eyes stole a glance sidelong at her strong fair lover. His face was white as death and set sternly before him, and his dishevelled hair and golden beard flowed wildly

over the rough coarseness of his long sackcloth garments. But his step never faltered, though he walked
barefooted upon the hard gravel, and from the upper
chamber of the tower whence they bore the corpse to
the very moment when they laid it in the tomb, his
face never changed, neither looked he to the right nor
to the left. And then, at last, when they had lowered
their beloved master with linen bands to his last
resting-place, and the women came near with boxes of
nard and ambergris and precious ointments, Zoroaster
looked long and fixedly at the swathed head, and the
tears rolled down his cheeks and dropped upon his
beard and upon the marble of the coffin; till at last
he turned in silence, and went away through the multitude that parted before him, as pale as the dead and
answering no man's greeting, nor even glancing at
Nehushta who had stood at his elbow. And he went
away and hid himself for the rest of that day.

But in the evening, when the sun was gone down,
he came and stood upon the terrace in the darkness,
for there was no moon. He wore again his arms, and
his purple cloak was about him, for he had his duty
to perform in visiting the fortress. The starlight
glimmered faintly on his polished helmet and duskily
made visible his marble features and his beard. He
stood with his back to the pillars of the balustrade,
looking towards the myrtles of the garden, for he knew
that Nehushta would come to the wonted tryst. He
waited long, but at last he heard a step upon the
gravel path and the rustle of the myrtles, and presently in the faint light he could see the white skirt
of her garment beneath the dark mantle moving swiftly
towards him. He sprang forward to meet her and
would have taken her in his arms, but she put him

back and looked away from him while she walked
slowly to the front of the terrace.   Even in the gloom
of the starlight Zoroaster could see that something had
offended her, and a cold weight seemed to fall upon his
breast and chilled the rising words of loving greeting.

Zoroaster followed her and laid his hand upon her
shoulder.   Unresponsive, she allowed it to remain
there.

"My beloved," he said at last, trying in vain to
look into her averted face, "have you no word for me
to-night?"   Still she answered nothing.   "Has your
sorrow made you forget our love?" he murmured close
to her ear.   She started back from him a little and
looked at him.   Even in the dusk he could see her
eyes flash as she answered:

"Had not your own sorrow so utterly got the mastery over you to-day that you even refused to look at
me?" she asked.   "In all that long hour when we
were so near together, did you give me one glance?
You had forgotten me in the extremity of your grief!"
she cried scornfully.   "And now that the first torrent
of your tears has dwindled to a little stream, you have
time to remember me!   I thank my lord for the
notice he deigns to give his handmaiden, but—I need
it not.   Well—why are you here?"

Zoroaster stood up to his height and folded his arms
deliberately, facing Nehushta, and he spoke calmly,
though there was in his voice the dulness of a great
and sudden pain.   He knew men well enough, but he
knew little of women.

"There is a time to be sorrowful and a time for
joy," he said.   "There is a time for weeping and a
time for the glances of love.   I did as I did, because
when a man has a great grief for one dead and when

he desires to show his sorrow in doing honour to one who has been as a father to him, it is not meet that other thoughts should be in his mind; not even those thoughts which are most dear to him and nearest to his heart. Therefore I looked not at you when we were burying our master, and though I love you and in my heart look ever on your face, yet to-day my eyes were turned from you and I saw you not. Wherefore are you angry with me?"

"I am not angry," said Nehushta, "but think you love me little that you turn from me so easily." She looked down, and her face was quite hidden in the dark shadow. Then Zoroaster put his arm about her neck and drew her to him, and, though she resisted a little, in a moment her head rested on his breast. Then she struggled again.

"Nay, let me go, for you do not love me!" she said, half in a whisper. But he held her close.

"Nay, but you shall not go, for I do love you," he answered tenderly.

"Shall not?" cried she, turning in his arms, half fiercely; then her voice sank and thrilled softly. "Say that I will not," she murmured, and her arms went round him and pressed him passionately to her. "Oh, my beloved, why do you ever seem so cold? so cold—when I so love you?"

"I am not cold," he said fondly, "and I love you beyond all power of words to tell. Said we not that you had your way and I mine? Who shall tell us which is the sweeter music when both unite in so grand a harmony? Only doubt not, for doubting is as the drop that falls from the eaves upon the marble corner-stone, and, by ever falling, wears furrows in the stone that the whole ocean could not soften."

"I will not doubt any more," said Nehushta suddenly, "only—can you not love me a little sometimes in the way I do you? It is so sweet,—my way of loving."

"Indeed I will try, for it is very sweet," answered Zoroaster, and, bending down, he kissed her lips. Far off from the tower the melancholy cry of an owl echoed sadly across the gardens, and a cool damp breeze sprang up suddenly from the east. Nehushta shuddered slightly, and drew her cloak about her.

"Let us walk upon the terrace," she said, "it is cold to-night—is not this the last night here?"

"Yes; to-morrow we must go hence upon our journey. This is the last night."

Nehushta drew closer to her lover as they paced the terrace together, and each wound one arm about the other. For some minutes they walked in silence, each perhaps recalling the many meetings upon that very terrace since the first time their lips met in love under the ivory moonlight of the month Tammuz, more than a year ago. At last Nehushta spoke.

"Know you this new king?" she asked. "I saw him but for a few moments last year. He was a young prince, but he is not fair."

"A young prince with an old man's head upon his shoulders," answered Zoroaster. "He is a year younger than I—but I would not have his battles to fight; nor, if I had, would I have taken Atossa to be my wife."

"Atossa?" repeated Nehushta.

"Yes. The king has already married her—she was the wife of Cambyses, and also of the false Smerdis, the Magian, whom Darius has slain."

"Is she fair? Have I not seen her?" asked Nehushta quickly.

"Indeed, you must have seen her at the court in Shushan, before we came to Ecbatana. She was just married to Cambyses then, but he regarded her little, for he was ever oppressed with wine and feasting. But you were a child then, and were mostly with the women of your house, and you may not have seen her."

"Tell me—had she not blue eyes and yellow hair? Had she not a cruel face—very cold?"

"Aye, it may be that she had a hard look. I remember that her eyes were blue. She was very unhappy; therefore she helped the Magian. It was not she that betrayed him."

"You pitied her even then, did you not?" asked Nehushta.

"Yes—she deserved pity."

"She will have her revenge now. A woman with a face like hers loves revenge."

"Then she will deserve pity no longer," said Zoroaster, with a slight laugh.

"I hate her!" said the princess, between her teeth.

"Hate her? How can you hate a woman you have never more than seen, and she has done you no evil in the world?"

"I am sure I shall hate her," answered Nehushta. "She is not at all beautiful—only cold and white and cruel. How could the Great King be so foolish as to marry her?"

"May he live for ever! He marries whom he pleases. But I pray you, do not begin by hating the queen overmuch."

"Why not? What have I to gain from the queen?" asked the princess. "Am I not of royal blood as well as she?"

"That is true," returned Zoroaster. "Nevertheless there is a prudence for princesses as well as for other people."

"I would not be afraid of the Great King himself with you beside me," said Nehushta proudly. "But I will be prudent to please you. Only—I am sure I shall hate her."

Zoroaster smiled to himself in the dusk, but he would not have had the princess see he was amused.

"It shall be as you please," he said; "we shall soon know how it will end, for we must begin our journey to-morrow."

"It will need three weeks, will it not?" asked Nehushta.

"Yes—it is at least one hundred and fifty farsangs. It would weary you to travel more than seven or eight farsangs in a day's journey—indeed, that is a long distance for any one."

"We shall always be together, shall we not?" asked the princess.

"I will ride beside your litter, my beloved," said Zoroaster. "But it will be very tedious for you, and you will often be tired. The country is very wild in some parts, and we must trust to what we can take with us for our comfort. Do not spare the mules therefore, but take everything you need."

"Besides, we may not return," said Nehushta thoughtfully.

Her companion was silent. "Do you think we shall ever come back?" she asked presently.

"I have dreamed of coming back," answered Zoroaster; "but I fear it is to be even as you say."

"Why say you that you fear it? Is it not better to live at the court than here in this distant fortress, so shut off from the world that we might almost as well be among the Scythians? Oh, I long for the palace at Shushan! I am sure it will seem tenfold more beautiful now than it did when I was a child."

Zoroaster sighed. In his heart he knew there was to be no returning to Media, and yet he had dreamed of marrying the princess and being made governor of the province, and bringing his wife home to this beautiful land to live out a long life of quiet happiness. But he knew it was not to be; and though he tried hard to shake off the impression, he felt in his inmost self that the words of the dying prophet foretold truly what would happen to him. Only he hoped that there was an escape, and the passion in his heart scorned the idea that in loving Nehushta he was being led astray, or made to abandon the right path.

The cold breeze blew steadily from the east, with a chill dampness in it, sighing wearily among the trees. The summer was not yet wholly come, and the afterbreath of the winter still made itself felt from time to time. The lovers parted, taking leave of the spot they loved so well,—Zoroaster with a heavy foreboding of evil to come; Nehushta with a great longing for the morrow, a mad desire to be on the way to Shushan.

Something in her way of speaking had given Zoroaster a sense of pain. Her interest in the court and in the Great King, the strange capricious hatred that seemed already forming in her breast against Atossa, the evident desire she betrayed to take part in the brilliant life of the capital,—indeed, her whole manner troubled him. It seemed so unaccountable that she should be angry with him for his conduct at the burial of the prophet, that he almost thought she had wished to take advantage of a trifle for the sake of annoying him. He felt that doubt which never comes so suddenly and wounds so keenly as when a man feels the most certain of his position and of himself.

He retired to his apartment in the palace with a burden of unhappiness and evil presentiment that was new to him. It was very different from the sincere sorrow he had felt and still suffered for the death of his master and friend. That misfortune had not affected him as regarded Nehushta. But now he had been separated from her during all the week by the exigencies of the funeral ceremonies, and he had looked forward to meeting her this evening as to a great joy after so much mourning, and he was disappointed. She had affected to be offended with him, yet his reason told him that he had acted naturally and rightly. Could he, the bearer of the prophet's body, the captain of all the fortress, the man of all others upon whom all eyes were turned, have exchanged love glances or spoken soft words to the princess by his side at such a time? It was absurd; she had no right to expect such a thing.

However, he reflected that a new kind of life was to begin on the morrow. For the best part of a month he would ride by her litter all day long, and sit at her table at noonday and evening; he would watch over her and take care of her, and see that her slightest wants were instantly supplied; a thousand incidents would occur whereby he might re-establish all the loving intimacy which seemed to have been so unexpectedly shaken. And so, consoling himself with the hopes of the future, and striving to overlook the present, he fell asleep, wearied with the fatigues and sorrows of the day.

But Nehushta lay all night upon her silken cushions, and watched the flickering little lamp and the strange shadows it cast among the rich, painted carvings of the ceiling. She slept little, but waking she dreamed of the gold and the glitter of Shushan, of the magnificence of the young king, and of the brilliant hard-featured beauty of Atossa, whom she already hated or had determined to hate. The king interested her most. She tried to recall his features and manner as he had appeared when he tarried one night in the fortress a year previous. She remembered a black-browed man in the prime of youth, with heavy brows and an eagle nose; his young beard growing black and square about his strong dark features, which would have seemed coarse saving for his bright eyes that looked every man fearlessly in the face. A short man he seemed in her memory, square built and powerful as a blood-hound, of quick and decisive speech, expecting to be understood before he had half spoken his thoughts; a man, she fancied, who must be untiring and violent of temper, inflexible and brave in the execution of his purpose—a strong contrast outwardly to her tall and graceful lover. Zoroaster's faultless beauty was a constant delight to her eyes; his soft deep voice sounded voluptuously passionate when he spoke to herself, coldly and deliberately dominating when addressing others. He moved with perfect certainty and assurance of purpose, his whole presence breathed a high and superior wisdom and untainted nobility of mind; he looked and acted like a god, like a being from another world, not subject to mortal passions, nor to the temptations of common mankind. She gloried in his perfection and in the secret knowledge that to her alone he was a man simply and utterly dominated by love.

As she thought of him she grew proud and happy in
the idea that such a man should be her lover, and she
reproached herself for doubting his devotion that evening.   After all, she had only complained that he had
neglected her—as he had really done, she added.   She
wondered in her heart whether other men would have
done the same in his place, or whether this power of
coldly disregarding her presence when he was occupied
with a serious matter were not due to a real and un-
conquerable hardness in his nature.

But as she lay there, her dark hair streaming over
the yellow silk of her pillows, her mind strayed from
her lover to the life before her, and the picture rose
quickly in her imagination.   She even took up the
silver mirror that lay beside her and looked at herself
by the dim light of the little lamp, and said to herself
that she was beautiful, and that many in Shushan
would do her homage.   She was glad that Atossa was
so fair—it would be a better contrast for her own dark
southern beauty.

Towards morning she slept, and dreamed of the
grand figure of the prophet, as she had seen him
stretched upon his death-bed in the upper chamber
of the tower; she thought the dead man stirred and
opened his glazed eyes and pointed at her with his
bony fingers, and spoke words of anger and reproach.
Then she woke with a short cry in her terror, and the
light of the dawn shone gray and clear through the
doorway of the corridor at the end of her room,
where two of her handmaids slept across the threshold,
their white cloaks drawn over their heads against the
chill air of the night.

Then the trumpets rang out in long-drawn clanging
rhythm through the morning air, and Nehushta heard

the trampling of the beasts that were being got ready
for the journey, in the court without, and the cries of
the drivers and of the serving-men.   She rose quickly
from her bed—a lithe white-clad figure in the dawn
light—and pushed the heavy curtains aside and looked
out through the lattice; and she forgot her evil dream,
for her heart. leaped again at the thought that she
should no more be shut up in Ecbatana, and that before another month was over she would be in Shushan,
in the palace, where she longed to be.

CHAPTER V.

THE sun was almost setting, and his light was already turning to a golden glow upon the vast plain of Shushan, as the caravan of travellers halted for the last time. A few stades away the two mounds rose above the royal city like two tables out of the flat country; the lower one surmounted by the marble columns, the towers and turrets and gleaming architraves of the palace; and in front, upon the right, the higher elevation crowned by the dark and massive citadel of frowning walls and battlements. The place chosen for the halt was the point where the road from Nineveh, into which they had turned when about half-way from Ecbatana, joined the broad road from Babylon, near to the bridge. For some time they had followed the quiet stream of the Choaspes, and, looking across it, had watched how the fortress seemed to come forward and overhang the river, while the mound of the palace fell away to the background. The city itself was, of course, completely hidden from their view by the steep mounds, that looked as inaccessible as though they had been built of solid masonry.

Everything in the plain was green. Stade upon stade, and farsang upon farsang, the ploughed furrows stretched away to the west and south; the corn standing already green and high, and the fig-trees putting out their broad green leaves. Here and there in the level expanse of country the rays of the declining sun were reflected from the whitewashed walls of a farm-house; or in the farther distance lingered upon the burnt-brick buildings of an outlying village. Beyond the river, in the broad meadow beneath the turret-clad mound, half-naked, sunburnt boys drove home the small humped cows to the milking, scaring away, as they went, the troops of white horses that pastured in the same field, clapping their hands and crying out at the little black foals that ran and frisked by the side of their white dams. Here and there a broad-shouldered, bearded fisherman angled in the stream, or flung out a brown casting-net upon the placid waters, drawing it slowly back to the bank, with eyes intent upon the moving cords.

The caravan halted on the turf by the side of the dusty road; the mounted guards, threescore stalwart riders from the Median plains, fell back to make room for the travellers, and, springing to the ground, set about picketing and watering their horses—their brazen armour and scarlet and blue mantles blazing in a mass of rich colour in the evening sun; while their wild white horses, untired by the day's march, plunged and snorted, and shook themselves, and bit each other in play by mane and tail, in the delight of being at least half free.

Zoroaster himself—his purple mantle somewhat whitened with the dust, and his fair face a little browned by the three weeks' journey—threw the bridle of his horse to a soldier and ran quickly forward. A magnificent litter, closed all around with a gilded lattice, and roofed with three awnings of white linen, one upon the other, as a protection against the sun,

was being carefully unyoked from the mules that had
borne it.   Tall Ethiopian slaves lifted it, and carried
it to the greenest spot of the turf by the softly flowing
river ; and Zoroaster himself pushed back the lattice
and spread a rich carpet before it.   Nehushta took
his proffered hand and stepped lightly out, and stood
beside him in the red light.   She was veiled, and her
purple cloak fell in long folds to her feet, and she
stood motionless, with her back to the city, looking
towards the setting sun.

"Why do we stop here?" she asked suddenly.

"The Great King, may he live for ever, is said not
to be in the city," answered Zoroaster, "and it would
ill become us to enter the palace before him."   He
spoke aloud in the Median language that the slaves
might hear him ; then he added in Hebrew and in a
lower voice, "It would be scarcely wise, or safe, to
enter Shushan when the king is away.   Who can
tell what may have happened there in these days ?
Babylon has rebelled ; the empire is far from settled.
All Persia may be on the very point of a revolt."

"A fitting time indeed for our journey—for me and
my women to be travelling abroad with a score of
horsemen for a guard !   Why did you bring me here?
How long are we to remain encamped by the roadside,
waiting the pleasure of the populace to let us in, or
the convenience of this new king to return?"

Nehushta turned upon her companion as she spoke,
and there was a ring of mingled scorn and disappointment in her voice.   Her dark eyes stared coldly at
Zoroaster from the straight opening between her veils,
and before he could answer, she turned her back upon
him and moved a few steps away, gazing out at the
setting sun across the fertile meadows.   The warrior

stood still, and a dark flush overspread his face. Then
he turned pale, but whatever were the words that rose
to his lips, he did not speak them, but occupied himself with superintending the pitching of the women's
tents. The other litters were brought, and set down
with their occupants; the long file of camels, some
laden with baggage and provisions, some bearing
female slaves, kneeled down to be unloaded upon
the grass, anxiously craning their long necks the
while in the direction of the stream; the tent-pitchers
set to work; and at the last another score of horsemen, who had formed the rear-guard of the caravan,
cantered up and joined their companions who had
already dismounted. With the rapid skill of long
practice, all did their share, and in a few minutes all
the immense paraphernalia of a Persian encampment
were spread out and disposed in place for the night.
Contrary to the usual habit Zoroaster had not permitted the tent-pitchers and other slaves to pass on
while he and his charges made their noonday halt;
for he feared some uprising in the neighbourhood of
the city in the absence of the king, and he wished to
keep his whole company together as a measure of
safety, even at the sacrifice of Nehushta's convenience.

She herself still stood apart, and haughtily turned
away from her serving-women, giving them no answer
when they saluted her and offered her cushions and
cooling drinks. She drew her cloak more closely
about her and tightened her veil upon her face. She
was weary, disappointed, almost angry. For days
she had dreamed of the reception she would have at
the palace, of the king and of the court; of the luxury
of rest after her long journey, and of the thousand
diversions and excitements she would find in revisiting

the scenes of her childhood. It was no small disappointment to find herself condemned to another
night in camp; and her first impulse was to blame
Zoroaster.

In spite of her love for him, her strong and dominating temper often chafed at his calmness, and resented the resolute superiority of his intelligence; and
then, being conscious that her own dignity suffered by
the storms of her temper, she was even more angry
than before, with herself, with him, with every one.
But Zoroaster was as impassive as marble, saving that
now and then his brow flushed, and paled quickly;
and his words, if he spoke at all, had a chilled icy
ring in them. Sooner or later, Nehushta's passionate
temper cooled, and she found him the same as ever,
devoted and gentle and loving; then her heart went
out to him anew, and all her being was filled with the
love of him, even to overflowing.

She had been disappointed now, and would speak
to no one. She moved still farther from the crowd of
slaves and tent-pitchers, followed at a respectful distance by her handmaidens, who whispered together
as they went; and again she stood still and looked
westward.

As the sun neared the horizon, his low rays caught
upon a rising cloud of dust, small and distant as the
smoke of a fire, in the plain towards Babylon, but
whirling quickly upwards. Nehushta's eye rested on
the far-off point, and she raised one hand to shade her
sight. She remembered how, when she was a girl, she
had watched the line of that very road from the palace
above, and had seen a cloud of dust arise out of a
mere speck, as a body of horsemen galloped into view.
There was no mistaking what it was. A troop of

horse were coming—perhaps the king himself. Instinctively she turned and looked for Zoroaster, and
started, as she saw him standing at a little distance
from her, with folded arms, his eyes bent on the
horizon. She moved towards him in sudden excitement.

"What is it?" she asked in low tones.

"It is the Great King—may he live for ever!"
answered Zoroaster. "None but he would ride so fast
along the royal road."

For a moment they stood side by side, watching the
dust cloud; and as they stood, Nehushta's hand stole
out from her cloak and touched the warrior's arm,
softly, with a trembling of the fingers, as though she
timidly sought something she would not ask for.
Zoroaster turned his head and saw that her eyes were
moistened with tears; he understood, but he would
not take her hand, for there were many slaves near,
besides Nehushta's kinsfolk, and he would not have
had them see; but he looked on her tenderly, and on
a sudden, his eyes grew less sad, and the light returned
in them.

"My beloved!" he said softly.

"I was wrong, Zoroaster—forgive me," she murmured. She suffered him to lead her to her tent,
which was already pitched; and he left her there,
sitting at the door and watching his movements, while
he called together his men and drew them up in a
compact rank by the roadside, to be ready to salute
the king.

Nearer and nearer came the cloud; and the red
glow turned to purple and the sun went out of sight;
and still it came nearer, that whirling cloud-canopy of
fine powdered dust, rising to right and left of the road

in vast round puffs, and hanging overhead like the
smoke from some great moving fire. Then, from beneath it, there seemed to come a distant roar like
thunder, rising and falling on the silent air, but rising
ever louder; and a dark gleam of polished bronze, with
something more purple than the purple sunset, took
shape slowly; then with the low roar of sound, came
now and then, and then more often, the clank of
harness and arms; till at last, the whole stamping,
rushing, clanging crowd of galloping horsemen seemed
to emerge suddenly from the dust in a thundering
charge, the very earth shaking beneath their weight,
and the whole air vibrating to the tremendous shock
of pounding hoofs and the din of clashing brass.

A few lengths before the serried ranks rode one
man alone,—a square figure, wrapped in a cloak of
deeper and richer purple than any worn by the ordinary
nobles, sitting like a rock upon a great white horse.
As he came up, Zoroaster and his fourscore men threw
up their hands.

"Hail, king of kings! Hail, and live for ever!"
they cried, and as one man, they prostrated themselves
upon their faces on the grass by the roadside.

Darius drew rein suddenly, bringing his steed from
his full gallop to his haunches in an instant. After
him the rushing riders threw up their right hands as a
signal to those behind; and with a deafening concus-
sion, as of the ocean breaking at once against a wall of
rock, those matchless Persian horsemen halted in a
body in the space of a few yards, their steeds plunging
wildly, rearing to their height and struggling on the
curb; but helpless to advance against the strong hands
that held them. The blossom and flower of all the
Persian nobles rode there,—their purple mantles flying

with the wild motion, their bronze cuirasses black in the gathering twilight, their bearded faces dark and square beneath their gilded helmets.

"I am Darius, the king of kings, on whom ye call," cried the king, whose steed now stood like a marble statue, immovable in the middle of the road. "Rise, speak and fear nothing,—unless ye speak lies."

Zoroaster rose to his feet, then bent low, and taking a few grains of dust from the roadside, touched his mouth with his hand and let the dust fall upon his forehead.

"Hail, and live for ever! I am thy servant, Zoroaster, who was captain over the fortress and treasury of Ecbatana. According to thy word I have brought the kinsfolk of Jehoiakim, king of Judah,—chief of whom is Nehushta, the princess. I heard that thou wast absent from Shushan, and here I have waited for thy coming. I also sent thee messengers to announce that Daniel, surnamed Belteshazzar, who was Satrap of Media from the time of Cambyses, is dead; and I have buried him fittingly in a new tomb in the garden of the palace of Ecbatana."

Darius, quick and impulsive in every thought and action, sprang to the ground as Zoroaster finished speaking, and coming to him, took both his hands and kissed him on both cheeks.

"What thou hast done is well done,—I know thee of old. Auramazda is with thee. He is also with me. By his grace I have slain the rebels at Babylon. They spoke lies, so I slew them. Show me Nehushta, the daughter of the kings of Judah."

"I am thy servant. The princess is at hand," answered Zoroaster; but as he spoke, he turned pale to the lips.

By this time it had grown dark, and the moon, just past the full, had not yet risen from behind the mound of the fortress. The slaves brought torches of mingled wax and fir-gum, and their black figures shone strangely in the red glare, as they pressed toward the door of Nehushta's tent, lighting the way for the king.

Darius strode quickly forward, his gilded harness clanging as he walked, the strong flaring light illuminating his bold dark features. Under the striped curtain, drawn up to form the entrance of the tent, stood Nehushta. She had thrown aside her veil and her women had quickly placed upon her head the linen tiara, where a single jewel shone like a star in the white folds. Her thick black hair fell in masses upon her shoulders, and her mantle was thrown back, displaying the grand proportions of her figure, clad in tunic and close-fitting belt. As the king came near, she kneeled and prostrated herself before him, touching her forehead to the ground, and waiting for him to speak.

He stood still a full minute and his eyes flashed fire, as he looked on her crouching figure, in very pride that so queenly a woman should be forced to kneel at his feet—but more in sudden admiration of her marvellous beauty. Then he bent down, and took her hand and raised her to her feet. She sprang up, and faced him with glowing cheeks and flashing eyes; and as she stood she was nearly as tall as he.

" I would not that a princess of thy line kneeled before me," said he; and in his voice there was a strange touch of softness. " Wilt thou let me rest here awhile before I go up to Shushan ? I am weary of riding and thirsty from the road."

" Hail, king of the world ! I am thy servant.

Rest thee and refresh thee here," answered Nehushta, drawing back into the tent. The king beckoned to Zoroaster to follow him and went in.

Darius sat upon the carved folding-chair that stood in the midst of the tent by the main pole, and eagerly drained the huge golden goblet of Shiraz wine which Zoroaster poured for him. Then he took off his head-piece, and his thick, coarse hair fell in a mass of dark curls to his neck, like the mane of a black lion. He breathed a long breath as of relief and enjoyment of well-earned repose, and leaned back in his chair, letting his eyes rest on Nehushta's face as she stood before him looking down to the ground. Zoroaster remained on one side, holding the replenished goblet in his hand, in case the king's thirst were not assuaged by a single draught.

"Thou art fair, daughter of Jerusalem," said the king presently. "I remember thy beauty, for I saw thee in Ecbatana. I sent for thee and thy kinsfolk that I might do thee honour; and I will also fulfil my words. I will take thee to be my wife."

Darius spoke quietly, in his usual tone of absolute determination. But if the concentrated fury of a thousand storms had suddenly broken loose in the very midst of the tent, the effect could not have been more terrible on his hearers.

Nehushta's face flushed suddenly, and for a moment she trembled in every joint; then she fell on her knees, prostrate before the king's feet, all the wealth of her splendid hair falling loose about her. Darius sat still, as though watching the result of his speech. He might have sat long, but in an instant, Zoroaster sprang between the king and the kneeling woman; and the golden goblet he had held rolled across the

F

thick carpet on the ground, while the rich red wine ran in a slow stream towards the curtains of the door. His face was livid and his eyes like coals of blue fire, his fair locks and his long golden beard caught the torchlight and shone about him like a glory, as he stood up to his grand height and faced the king. Darius never quailed nor moved; his look met Zoroaster's with fearless boldness. Zoroaster spoke first, in low accents of concentrated fury:

"Nehushta the princess is my betrothed bride. Though thou wert king of the stars as well as king of the earth, thou shalt not have her for thy wife."

Darius smiled, not scornfully, an honest smile of amusement, as he stared at the wrathful figure of the northern man before him.

"I am the king of kings," he answered. "I will marry this princess of Judah to-morrow, and thee I will crucify upon the highest turret of Shushan, because thou speakest lies when thou sayest I shall not marry her."

"Fool! tempt not thy God! Threaten not him who is stronger than thou, lest he slay thee with his hands where thou sittest." Zoroaster's voice sounded low and distinct as the knell of relentless fate, and his hand went out towards the king's throat.

Until this moment, Darius had sat in his indifferent attitude, smiling carelessly, though never taking his eye from his adversary. Brave as the bravest, he scorned to move until he was attacked, and he would have despised the thought of calling to his guards. But when Zoroaster's hand went out to seize him, he was ready. With a spring like a tiger, he flew at the strong man's throat, and sought to drag him down, striving to fasten his grip about the collar of his cuirass, but Zoroaster slipped his hand quickly under his adversary's, his sleeve went back and his long white arm ran like a fetter of steel about the king's neck, while his other hand gripped him by the middle; so they held each other like wrestlers, one arm above the shoulder and one below, and strove with all their might.

The king was short, but in his thick-set broad shoulders and knotted arms there lurked the strength of a bull and the quickness of a tiger. Zoroaster had the advantage, for his right arm was round Darius's neck, but while one might count a score, neither moved a hairbreadth, and the blue veins stood out like cords on the tall man's arm. The fiery might of the southern prince was matched against the stately strength of the fair northerner, whose face grew as white as death, while the king's brow was purple with the agony of effort. They both breathed hard between their clenched teeth, but neither uttered a word.

Nehushta had leaped to her feet in terror at the first sign of the coming strife, but she did not cry out, nor call in the slaves or guards. She stood, holding the tent-pole with one hand, and gathering her mantle to her breast with the other, gazing in absolute fascination at the fearful life and death struggle, at the unspeakable and tremendous strength so silently exerted by the two men before her.

Suddenly they moved and swayed. Darius had attempted to trip Zoroaster with one foot, but slipping on the carpet wet with wine, had been bent nearly double to the ground; then by a violent effort, he regained his footing. But the great exertion had weakened his strength. Nehushta thought a smile flickered on Zoroaster's pale face and his flashing dark blue eyes met hers for a moment, and then the end

began. Slowly, and by imperceptible degrees, Zoroaster forced the king down before him, doubling him
backwards with irresistible strength, till it seemed as
though bone and sinew and muscle must be broken
and torn asunder in the desperate resistance. Then,
at last, when his head almost touched the ground,
Darius groaned and his limbs relaxed. Instantly
Zoroaster threw him on his back and kneeled with his
whole weight upon his chest,—the gilded scales of the
corslet cracking beneath the burden, and he held the
king's hands down on either side, pinioned to the floor.
Darius struggled desperately twice and then lay quite
still. Zoroaster gazed down upon him with blazing
eyes.

" Thou who wouldst crucify me upon Shushan," he
said through his teeth. " I will slay thee here even
as thou didst slay Smerdis. Hast thou anything to
say ? Speak quickly, for thy hour is come."

Even in the extremity of his agony, vanquished and
at the point of death, Darius was brave, as brave men
are, to the very last. He would indeed have called
for help now, but there was no breath in him. He
still gazed fearlessly into the eyes of his terrible conqueror. His voice came in a hoarse whisper.

" I fear not death. Slay on if thou wilt—thou—
hast—conquered."

Nehushta had come near. She trembled now that
the fight was over, and looked anxiously to the heavy
curtains of the tent-door.

" Tell him," she whispered to Zoroaster, " that you
will spare him if he will do no harm to you, nor to
me."

" Spare him !" echoed Zoroaster scornfully. " He
is almost dead now—why should I spare him ? "

"For my sake, beloved," answered Nehushta, with a sudden and passionate gesture of entreaty. "He is the king—he speaks truth; if he says he will not harm you, trust him."

"If I slay thee not, swear thou wilt not harm me nor Nehushta," said Zoroaster, removing one knee from the chest of his adversary.

"By the name of Auramazda," gasped Darius, " I will not harm thee nor her."

"It is well," said Zoroaster. "I will let thee go. And as for taking her to be thy wife, thou mayest ask her if she will wed thee," he added. He rose and helped the king to his feet. Darius shook himself and breathed hard for a few minutes. He felt his limbs as a man might do who had fallen from his horse, and then he sat down upon the chair, and broke into a loud laugh.

Darius was well known to all Persia and Media before the events of the last two months, and such was his reputation for abiding by his promise that he was universally trusted by those about him. Zoroaster had known him also, and he remembered his easy familiarity and love of jesting, so that even when he held the king at such vantage that he might have killed him by a little additional pressure of his weight, he felt not the least hesitation in accepting his promise of safety. But remembering what a stake had been played for in the desperate issue, he could not join in the king's laugh. He stood silently apart, and looked at Nehushta who leaned back against the tent-pole in violent agitation; her hands wringing each other beneath her long sleeves, and her eyes turning from the king to Zoroaster, and back again to the king, in evident distress and fear.

"Thou hast a mighty arm, Zoroaster," cried Darius, as his laughter subsided, "and thou hadst well-nigh made an end of the Great King and of Persia, Media, Babylon and Egypt in thy grip."

"Let the king pardon his servant," answered Zoroaster, "if his knee was heavy and his hand strong. Had not the king slipped upon the spilt wine, his servant would have been thrown down."

"And thou wouldst have been crucified at dawn," added Darius, laughing again. "It is well for thee that I am Darius and not Cambyses, or thou wouldst not be standing there before me while my guards are gossiping idly in the road. Give me a cup of wine since thou hast spared my life!" Again the king laughed as though his sides would break. Zoroaster hastily filled another goblet and offered it, kneeling before the monarch. Darius paused before he took the cup, and looked at the kneeling warrior's pale proud face. Then he spoke and his voice dropped to a less mirthful key, as he laid his hand on Zoroaster's shoulder.

"I love thee, prince," he said, "because thou art stronger than I; and as brave and more merciful. Therefore shalt thou stand ever at my right hand and I will trust thee with my life in thy hand. And in pledge hereunto I put my own chain of gold about thy neck, and I drink this cup to thee; and whosoever shall harm a hair of thine head shall perish in torments."

The king drank; and Zoroaster, overcome with genuine admiration of the great soul that could so easily forgive so dire an offence, bent and embraced the king's knees in token of adherence, and as a seal of that friendship which was never to be broken until death parted the two men asunder.

Then they arose, and at Zoroaster's order, the

princess's litter was brought, and leaving the encampment to follow after them, they went up to the palace. Nehushta was borne between the litters of her women and her slaves on foot, but Zoroaster mounted his horse and rode slowly and in silence by the right side of the Great King.

CHAPTER VI.

ATHWART the gleaming colonnades of the eastern
balcony, the early morning sun shone brightly, and all
the shadows of the white marble cornices and capitals
and jutting frieze work were blue with the reflection of
the cloudless sky. The swallows now and then shot
in under the overhanging roof and flew up and down
the covered terrace; then with a quick rush, they sped
forth again into the dancing sunshine with clean sudden
sweep, as when a sharp sword is whirled in the air.
Far below, the soft mist of the dawn still lay upon the
city, whence the distant cries of the water-carriers and
fruitsellers came echoing up from the waking streets,
the call of the women to one another from the house-
tops, and now and then the neighing of a horse far out
upon the meadows; while the fleet swallows circled
over all in swift wide curves, with a silvery fresh
stream of unceasing twittering music.

Zoroaster paced the balcony alone. He was fully
armed, with his helmet upon his head; the crest of
the winged wheels was replaced by the ensign Darius
had chosen for himself,—the half-figure of a likeness
of the king with long straight wings on either side, of
wrought gold and very fine workmanship. The long
purple mantle hung to his heels and the royal chain
of gold was about his neck. As he walked the gilded

leather of his shoes was reflected in the polished marble pavement and he trod cautiously, for the clean surface was slippery as the face of a mirror. At one end of the terrace a stairway led down to the lower story of the palace, and at the other end a high square door was masked by a heavy curtain of rich purple and gold stuff, that fell in thick folds to the glassy floor. Each time his walk brought him to this end Zoroaster paused, as though expecting that some one should come out. But as it generally happens when a man is waiting for something or some one that the object or person appears unexpectedly, so it occurred that as he turned back from the staircase towards the curtain, he saw that some one had already advanced half the length of the balcony to meet him—and it was not the person for whom he was looking.

At first, he was dazzled for a moment, but his memory served him instantly and he recognised the face and form of a woman he had known and often seen before. She was not tall, but so perfectly proportioned that it was impossible to wish that she were taller. Her close tunic of palest blue, bordered with a gold embroidery at the neck, betrayed the matchless symmetry of her figure, the unspeakable grace of development of a woman in the fullest bloom of beauty. From her knees to her feet, her under tunic showed the purple and white bands that none but the king might wear, and which even for the queen was an undue assumption of the royal insignia. But Zoroaster did not look at her dress, nor at her mantle of royal sea-purple, nor at the marvellous white hands that held together a written scroll. His eyes rested on her face, and he stood still where he was.

He knew those straight and perfect features, not

large nor heavy, but of such rare mould and faultless
type as man has not seen since, neither will see. The
perfect curve of the fresh mouth; the white forward
chin with its sunk depression in the midst; the deep-set,
blue eyes and the straight pencilled brows; the broad
smooth forehead and the tiny ear half hidden in the
glory of sun-golden hair; the milk-white skin just
tinged with the faint rose-light that never changed or
reddened in heat or cold, in anger or in joy—he knew
them all; the features of royal Cyrus made soft and
womanly in substance, but unchanging still and fault-
lessly cold in his great daughter Atossa, the child of
kings, the wife of kings, the mother of kings.

The heavy curtains had fallen together behind her,
and she came forward alone. She had seen Zoroaster
before he had seen her, and she moved on without
showing any surprise, the heels of her small golden
shoes clicking sharply on the polished floor. Zoroaster
remained standing for a moment, and then, removing
his helmet in salutation, went to one side of the head
of the staircase and waited respectfully for the queen
to pass. As she came on, passing alternately through
the shadow cast by the columns, and the sunlight that
blazed between, her advancing figure flashed with a
new illumination at every step. She made as though
she were going straight on, but as she passed over the
threshold to the staircase, she suddenly stopped and
turned half round, and looked straight at Zoroaster.

"Thou art Zoroaster," she said in a smooth and
musical voice, like the ripple of a clear stream flowing
through summer meadows.

"I am Zoroaster, thy servant," he answered, bowing
his head. He spoke very coldly.

"I remember thee well," said the queen, lingering

by the head of the staircase. "Thou art little changed,
saving that thou art stronger, I should think, and more
of a soldier than formerly."

Zoroaster stood turning his polished helmet in his
hands, but he answered nothing; he cared little for
the queen's praises. But she, it seemed, was desirous
of pleasing him in proportion as he was less anxious
to be pleased, for she turned again and walked forward
upon the terrace.

"Come into the sunlight—the morning air is cold,"
she said, "I would speak with thee awhile."

A carved chair stood in a corner of the balcony.
Zoroaster moved it into the sunshine, and Atossa sat
down, smiling her thanks to him, while he stood leaning against the balustrade,—a magnificent figure as the
light caught his gilded harness and gold neck-chain,
and played on his long fair beard and nestled in the
folds of his purple mantle.

"Tell me—you came last night?" she asked, spreading her dainty hands in the sunshine as though to
warm them. She never feared the sun, for he was
friendly to her nativity and never seemed to scorch
her fair skin like that of meaner women.

"Thy servant came last night," answered the prince.

"Bringing Nehushta and the other Hebrews?"
added the queen.

"Even so."

"Tell me something of this Nehushta," said Atossa.
She had dropped into a more familiar form of speech.
But Zoroaster was careful of his words and never
allowed his language to relapse from the distant form
of address of a subject to his sovereign.

"The queen knoweth her. She was here as a young
child a few years since," he replied. He chose to

let Atossa ask questions for all the information she
needed.

"It is so long ago," she said, with a little sigh. "Is
she fair?"

"Nay, she is dark, after the manner of the Hebrews."

"And the Persians too," she interrupted.

"She is very beautiful," continued Zoroaster. "She
is very tall." Atossa looked up quickly with a smile.
She was not tall herself, with all her beauty.

"You admire tall women?"

"Yes," said Zoroaster calmly—well knowing what
he said. He did not wish to flatter the queen; and
besides he knew her too well to do so if he wished to
please her. She was one of those women who are not
accustomed to doubt their own superiority over the
rest of their sex.

"Then you admire this Hebrew princess?" said she,
and paused for an answer. But her companion was as
cold and calm as she. Seeing himself directly pressed
by a suspicion, he changed his tactics and flattered
Atossa for the sake of putting a stop to her questions.

"Height is not of itself beauty," he answered with a
courteous smile. "There is a kind of beauty which
no height can improve,—a perfection which needs not
to be set high for all men to acknowledge it."

The queen simply took no notice of the compliment,
but it had its desired effect, for she changed the tone
of her talk a little, speaking more seriously.

"Where is she? I will go and see her," she said.

"She rested last night in the upper chambers in the
southern part of the palace. Thy servant will bid her
come if it be thy desire."

"Presently, presently," answered the queen. "It is
yet early, and she was doubtless weary of the journey."

There was a pause. Zoroaster looked down at the beautiful queen as she sat beside him, and wondered whether she had changed; and as he gazed, he fell to comparing her beauty with Nehushta's, and his glance grew more intent than he had meant it should be, so that Atossa looked up suddenly and met his eyes resting on her face.

"It is long since we have met, Zoroaster," she said quickly. "Tell me of your life in that wild fortress. You have prospered in your profession of arms—you wear the royal chain." She put up her hand and touched the links as though to feel them. "Indeed it is very like the chain Darius wore when he went to Babylon the other day." She paused a moment as though trying to recall something; then continued: "Yes—now I think of it, he had no chain when he came back. It is his—of course—why has he given it to you?" Her tones had a tinge of uncertainty in the question, —half imperious, as demanding an answer, half persuading, as though not sure the answer would be given. Zoroaster remembered that intonation of her sweet voice, and he smiled in his beard.

"Indeed," he answered, "the Great King who liveth for ever, put this chain about my neck with his own hands last night, when he halted by the roadside, as a reward, I presume, for certain qualities he believeth his servant Zoroaster to possess."

"Qualities—what qualities?"

"Nay, the queen cannot expect me to sing faithfully my own praises. Nevertheless, I am ready to die for the Great King. He knoweth that I am. May he live for ever!"

"It may be that one of the qualities was the successful performance of the extremely difficult task you have lately accomplished," said Atossa, with a touch of scorn.

"A task?" repeated Zoroaster.

"Yes—have you not brought a handful of Hebrew women all the way from Ecbatana to Shushan, through numberless dangers and difficulties, safe and sound, and so carefully prudent of their comfort that they are not even weary, nor have they once hungered or thirsted by the way, nor lost the smallest box of perfume, nor the tiniest of their golden hair-pins? Surely you have deserved to have a royal chain hung about your neck and to be called the king's friend."

"The reward was doubtless greater than my desert. It was no great feat of arms that I had to perform; and yet, in these days a man may leave Media under one king, and reach Shushan under another. The queen knoweth better than any one what sudden changes may take place in the empire," answered Zoroaster, looking calmly into her face as he stood; and she who had been the wife of Cambyses and the wife of the murdered Gomata-Smerdis, and who was now the wife of Darius, looked down and was silent, turning over in her beautiful hands the sealed scroll she bore.

The sun had risen higher while they talked, and his rays were growing hot in the clear air. The mist had lifted from the city below, and all the streets and open places were alive with noisy buyers and sellers, whose loud talking and disputing came up in a continuous hum to the palace on the hill, like the drone of a swarm of bees. The queen rose from her seat.

"It is too warm here," she said, and she once more moved toward the stairway. Zoroaster followed her respectfully, still holding his helmet in his hand. Atossa did not speak till she reached the threshold.

Then, as Zoroaster bowed low before her, she paused and looked at him with her clear, deep-blue eyes.

"You have grown very formal in four years," she said softly. "You used to be more outspoken and less of a courtier. I am not changed—we must be friends as we were formerly."

Zoroaster hesitated a moment before he answered:

"I am the Great King's man," he said slowly. "I am, therefore, also the queen's servant."

Atossa raised her delicate eyebrows a little and a shade of annoyance passed for the first time over her perfect face, which gave her a look of sternness.

"I am the queen," she said coldly. "The king may take other wives, but I am the queen. Take heed that you be indeed my servant." Then, as she gathered her mantle about her and put one foot upon the stairs, she touched his shoulder gently with the tips of her fingers and added with a sudden smile, "And I will be your friend." So she passed down the stairs out of sight, leaving Zoroaster alone.

Slowly he paced the terrace again, reflecting profoundly upon his situation. Indeed he had no small cause for anxiety; it was evident that the queen suspected his love for Nehushta, and he was more than half convinced that there were reasons why such an affection would inevitably meet with her disapproval. In former days, before she was married to Cambyses, and afterwards, before Zoroaster had been sent into Media, Atossa had shown so marked a liking for him, that a man more acquainted with the world, would have guessed that she loved him. He had not suspected such a thing, but with a keen perception of character, he had understood that beneath the beautiful features and the frank gentleness of the young princess, there

lurked a profound intelligence, an unbending ambition
and a cold selfishness without equal; he had mistrusted
her, but he had humoured her caprices and been in
truth a good friend to her, without in the least wishing
to accept her friendship for himself in return. He was
but a young captain of five hundred then, although he
was the favourite of the court; but his strong arm was
dreaded as well as the cutting force of his replies when
questioned, and no word of the court gossip had therefore reached his ears concerning Atossa's admiration
for him. It was, moreover, so evident that he cared
nothing for her beyond the most unaffected friendliness,
that her disappointment in not moving his heart was
a constant source of satisfaction to her enemies. There
had reigned in those days a great and unbridled license
in the court, and the fact of the daughter of Cyrus
loving and being loved by the handsomest of the king's
guards, would not of itself have attracted overmuch
notice. But the evident innocence of Zoroaster in the
whole affair, and the masterly fashion in which Atossa
concealed her anger, if she felt any, caused the matter
to be completely forgotten as soon as Zoroaster left
Shushan, and events had, since then, succeeded each
other too rapidly to give the courtiers leisure for gossiping about old scandals. The isolation in which Gomata
had lived during the seven months while he maintained
the popular impression that he was not Gomata-Smerdis,
but Smerdis the brother of Cambyses, had broken up
the court; and the strong, manly character of Darius
had checked the license of the nobles suddenly, as a
horse-breaker brings up an unbroken colt by flinging
the noose about his neck. The king permitted that
the ancient custom of marrying as many as four wives
should be maintained, and he himself soon set an

example by so doing; but he had determined that the whole corrupt fabric of court life should be shattered at one blow; and with his usual intrepid disregard of consequences and his iron determination to maintain his opinions, he had suffered no contradiction of his will.   He had married Atossa,—in the first place, because she was the most beautiful woman in Persia; and secondly, because he comprehended her great intelligence and capacity for affairs, and believed himself able to make use of her at his pleasure.   As for Atossa herself, she had not hesitated a moment in concurring in the marriage,—she had ruled her former husbands, and she would rule Darius in like manner, she thought, to her own complete aggrandisement and in the face of all rivals.   As yet, the king had taken no second wife, although he looked with growing admiration upon the maiden Artystoné, who was then but fifteen years of age, the youngest daughter of Cyrus and own sister to Atossa.

All this Zoroaster knew, and he recognised also from the meeting he had just had with the queen, that she was desirous of maintaining her friendship with himself.   But since the violent scene of the previous night, he had determined to be the king's man in truest loyalty, and he feared lest Atossa's plans might, before long, cross her husband's.   Therefore he accepted her offer of friendship coldly, and treated her with the most formal courtesy.   On the other hand, he understood well enough that if she resented his manner of acting towards her, and ascertained that he really loved Nehushta, it would be in her power to produce difficulties and complications which he would have every cause for fearing.   She would certainly discover the king's admiration for Nehushta.   Darius was a man

almost incapable of concealment; with whom to think
was to act instantly and without hesitation. He generally acted rightly, for his instincts were noble and
kingly, and his heart as honest and open as the very
light of day. He said what he thought and instantly
fulfilled his words. He hated a lie as poison, and the
only untruth he had ever been guilty of was told when,
in order to gain access to the dwelling of the false
Smerdis, he had declared to the guards that he brought
news of importance from his father. He had justified
this falsehood by the most elaborate and logical apology
to his companions, the six princes, and had explained
that he only lied for the purpose of saving Persia;
and when the lot fell to himself to assume the royal
authority, he fulfilled most amply every promise he
had given of freeing the country from tyranny, religious
despotism and, generally, from what he termed "lies."
As for the killing of Gomata-Smerdis, it was an act
of public justice, approved by all sensible persons as
soon as it was known by what frauds that impostor
had seized the kingdom.

With regard to Atossa, Darius had abstained from
asking her questions about her seven months of
marriage with the usurper. She must have known
well enough who the man was, but Darius understood
her character well enough to know that she would
marry whomsoever she saw in the chief place, and
that her counsel and courage would be of inestimable
advantage to a ruler. She herself never mentioned
the past events to the king, knowing his hatred of lies
on the one hand, and that on the other, the plain truth
would redound to her discredit. He had given her to
understand as much from the first, telling her that he
took her for what she was, and not for what she had

been. Her mind was at rest about the past, and as for the future, she promised herself her full share in her husband's success, should he succeed, and unbounded liberty in the choice of his successor, should he fail.

But all these considerations did not tend to clear Zoroaster's vision in regard to his own future. He saw himself already placed in a position of extreme difficulty between Nehushta and the king. On the other hand, he dreaded lest he should before long fall into disgrace with the king on account of Atossa's treatment of himself, or incur Atossa's displeasure through the great favour he received from Darius. He knew the queen to be an ambitious woman, capable of the wildest conceptions, and possessed of the utmost skill for their execution.

He longed to see Nehushta and talk with her at once,—to tell her many things and to warn her of many possibilities; above all, he desired to discuss with her the scene of the previous night and the strangely sudden determination the king had expressed to make her his wife.

But he could not leave his post. His orders had been to await the king in the morning upon the eastern terrace; and there he must abide until it pleased Darius to come forth; and he knew Nehushta would not venture down into that part of the palace. He wondered that the king did not come, and he chafed at the delay as he saw the sun rising higher and higher, and the shadows deepening in the terrace. Weary of waiting he sat down at last upon the chair where Atossa had rested, and folded his hands over his sword-hilt,—resigning himself to the situation with the philosophy of a trained soldier.

Sitting thus alone, he fell to dreaming. As he gazed out at the bright sky, he forgot his life and his love, and all things of the present; and his mind wandered away among the thoughts most natural and most congenial to his profound intellect. His attention became fixed in the contemplation of a larger dimension of intelligences,—the veil of darkness parted a little, and for a time he saw clearly in the light of a Greater Universe.

CHAPTER VII.

ATOSSA quitted the terrace where she had been talking with Zoroaster, in the full intention of returning
speedily, but as she descended the steps, a plan formed
itself in her mind, which she determined to put into
immediate execution.   Instead, therefore, of pursuing
her way into the portico of the inner court, when she
reached the foot of the staircase, she turned into a
narrow passage that led into a long corridor, lighted
only by occasional small openings in the wall.   A little
door gave access to this covered way, and when she
entered, she closed it behind her, and tried to fasten it.
But the bolt was rusty, and in order to draw it, she
laid down the scroll she carried, upon a narrow stone
seat by the side of the door; and then, with a strong
effort of both her small white hands, she succeeded in
moving the lock into its place.   Then she turned
quickly and hastened down the dusky corridor.   At
the opposite end a small winding stair led upwards
into darkness.   There were stains upon the lowest
steps, just visible in the half light.   Atossa gathered
up her mantle and her under tunic, and trod daintily,
with a look of repugnance on her beautiful face.   The
stains were made by the blood of the false Smerdis,
her last husband, slain in that dark stairway by Darius,
scarcely three months before.

Cautiously the queen felt her way upward till she reached a landing, where a narrow aperture admitted a little light. Higher up there were windows, and she looked carefully to her dress, and brushed away a little dust that her mantle had swept from the wall in passing; and once or twice, she looked back at the dark staircase with an expression of something akin to disgust. At last she reached a door which opened upon a terrace, much like the one where she had left Zoroaster a few moments before, saving that the floor was less polished, and that the spaces between the columns were half filled with hanging plants and creepers. Upon the pavement at one end were spread rich carpets, and half a dozen enormous cushions of soft-coloured silk were thrown negligently one upon the other. Three doors, hung with curtains, opened upon the balcony,—and near to the middle one, two slave-girls, clad in white, crouched upon their heels and talked in an undertone.

Atossa stepped forward upon the marble, and the rustle of her dress and the quick short sound of her heeled shoes, roused the two slave-girls to spring to their feet. They did not know the queen, but they thought it best to make a low obeisance, while their dark eyes endeavoured quickly to scan the details of her dress, without exhibiting too much boldness. Atossa beckoned to one of them to come to her, and smiled graciously as the dark-skinned girl approached.

"Is not thy mistress Nehushta?" she inquired; but the girl looked stupidly at her, not comprehending her speech. "Nehushta," repeated the queen, pronouncing the name very distinctly with a questioning intonation, and pointing to the curtained door. The slave understood the name and the question, and quick as thought, she disappeared within, leaving Atossa in some hesitation. She had not intended to send for the Hebrew princess, for she thought it would be a greater compliment to let Nehushta find her waiting; but since the barbarian slave had gone to call her mistress, there was nothing to be done but to abide the result.

Nehushta, however, seemed in no hurry to answer the summons, for the queen had ample time to examine the terrace, and to glance through the hanging plants at the sunlit meadows and the flowing stream to southward, before she heard steps behind the curtain, and saw it lifted to allow the princess to pass.

The dark maiden was now fully refreshed and rested from the journey, and she came forward to greet her guest in her tunic, without her mantle, a cloud of soft white Indian gauze loosely pinned upon her black hair and half covering her neck. Her bodice-like belt was of scarlet and gold, and from one side there hung a rich-hilted knife of Indian steel in a jewelled sheath. The long sleeves of her tunic were drawn upon her arms into hundreds of minute folds, and where the delicate stuff hung in an oblong lappet over her hands, there was fine needlework and embroidery of gold. She moved easily, with a languid grace of secure motion; and she bent her head a little as Atossa came quickly to meet her.

The queen's frank smile was on her face as she grasped both Nehushta's hands in cordial welcome, and for a moment, the two women looked into each other's eyes. Nehushta had made up her mind to hate Atossa from the first, but she did not belong to that class of women who allow their feelings to show themselves, and afterwards feel bound by the memory of what they have shown. She, too, smiled most sweetly as she

surveyed the beautiful fair queen from beneath her
long drooping lids, and examined her appearance with
all possible minuteness.   She remembered her well
enough, but so warm was the welcome she received,
that she almost thought she had misjudged Atossa in
calling her hard and cold.   She drew her guest to the
cushions upon the carpets, and they sat down side by
side.

"I have been talking about you already this morning,
my princess," began Atossa, speaking at once in familiar
terms, as though she were conversing with an intimate
friend.   Nehushta was very proud; she knew herself
to be of a race as royal as Atossa, though now almost
extinct; and in answering, she spoke in the same
manner as the queen; so that the latter was inwardly
amused at the self-confidence of the Hebrew princess.

"Indeed?" said Nehushta, "there must be far more
interesting things than I in Shushan.   I would have
talked of you had I found any one to talk with."

The queen laughed a little.

"As I was coming out this morning, I met an old
friend of mine upon the balcony before the king's
apartment,—Zoroaster, the handsome captain.   We fell
into conversation.   How handsome he has grown since
I saw him last!"   The queen watched Nehushta closely
while affecting the greatest unconcern, and she thought
the shadows about the princess's eyes turned a shade
darker at the mention of the brilliant warrior.   But
Nehushta answered calmly enough:

"He took the most excellent care of us.   I should
like to see him to-day, to thank him for all he did.   I
was tired last night and must have seemed ungrateful."

"What need is there of ever telling men we are
grateful for what they do for us?" returned the queen.

"I should think there were not a noble in the Great King's guard who would not give his right hand to take care of you for a month, even if you never so much as noticed his existence."

Nehushta laughed lightly at the compliment.

"You honour me too much," she said, "but I suppose it is because most women think as you do that men call us so ungrateful. I think you judge from the standpoint of the queen, whereas I——"

"Whereas you look at things from the position of the beautiful princess, who is worshipped for herself alone, and not for the bounty and favour she may, or may not, dispense to her subjects."

"The queen is dispensing much bounty and favour to one of her subjects at this very moment," answered Nehushta quietly, as though deprecating further flattery.

"How glad you must be to have left that dreadful fortress at last!" cried the queen sympathetically. "My father used to go there every summer. I hated the miserable place, with those tiresome mountains and those endless gardens without the least variety in them. You must be very glad to have come here!"

"It is true," replied Nehushta, "I never ceased to dream of Shushan. I love the great city, and the people, and the court. I thought sometimes that I should have died of the weariness of Ecbatana. The winters were unbearable!"

"You must learn to love us, too," said Atossa, very sweetly.. "The Great King wishes well to your race, and will certainly do much for your country. There is, moreover, a kinsman of yours, who is coming soon, expressly to confer with the king concerning the further rebuilding of the temple and the city of Jerusalem."

"Zorobabel?" asked Nehushta, quickly.

"Yes—that is his name, I believe. Do you say Zerub-Ebel, or Zerub-Abel? I know nothing of your language."

"His name is Zorob-Abel," answered Nehushta. "Oh, I wish he might persuade the Great King to do something for my people! Your father would have done so much if he had lived."

"Doubtless the Great King will do all that is possible for establishing the Hebrews and promoting their welfare," said the queen; but a distant look in her eyes showed that her thoughts were no longer concentrated on the subject. "Your friend Zoroaster," she added presently, "could be of great service to you and your cause, if he wished."

"I would that he were a Hebrew!" exclaimed Nehushta, with a little sigh, which did not escape Atossa.

"Is he not? I always thought that he had secretly embraced your faith. With his love of study and with his ideas, it seemed so natural."

"No," replied Nehushta, "he is not one of us, nor will he ever be. After all, though, it is perhaps of little moment what one believes when one is so just as he."

"I have never been able to understand the importance of religion," said the beautiful queen, spreading her white hand upon the purple of her mantle, and contemplating its delicate outline tenderly. "For my own part, I am fond of the sacrifices and the music and the chants. I love to see the priests go up to the altar, two and two, in their white robes,—and then to see how they struggle to hold up the bullock's head, so that his eyes may see the sun,—and how the red blood gushes out like a beautiful fountain. Have you ever seen a great sacrifice?"

" Oh yes! I remember when I was quite a little
girl, when Cambyses—I mean—when the king came
to the throne—it was magnificent!" Nehushta was
not used to hesitate in her speech, but as she recalled
the day when Cambyses was made king, it suddenly
came over her that any reminiscences of the past might
be painful to the extraordinary woman by her side.
But Atossa showed no signs of being disturbed. On
the contrary, she smiled more sweetly than ever, though
there was perhaps a slight affectation of sadness in her
voice as she answered:

" Do not fear to hurt me by referring to those times,
dear princess. I am accustomed to speak of them well
enough. Yes, indeed I remember that great day, with
the bright sun shining upon the procession, and the
cars with four horses that they dedicated to the sun,
and the milk-white horse that they slaughtered upon
the steps of the temple. How I cried for him, poor
beast! It seemed so cruel to sacrifice a horse! Even
a few black slaves would have been a more natural
offering, or a couple of Scythians."

" I remember," said Nehushta, somewhat relieved at
the queen's tone. " Of course I have now and then
seen processions in Ecbatana, but Daniel would not let
me go to the temple. They say Ecbatana is very much
changed since the Great King has not gone there in
summer. It is very quiet—it is given over to horse-
merchants and grain-sellers, and they bring all the
salted fish there from the Hyrcanian sea, so that some
of the streets smell horribly."

Atossa laughed at the description, more out of
courtesy than because it amused her.

" In my time," she answered, " the horse-market was
in the meadow by the road towards Zagros, and the

fish-sellers were not allowed to come within a farsang of the city. The royal nostrils were delicate. But everything is changed—here, everywhere. We have had several—revolutions—religious ones, I mean of course, and so many people have been killed that there is a savour of death in the air. It is amazing how much trouble people will give themselves about the question of sacrificing a horse to the sun, or a calf to Auramazda, or an Ethiopian to Nabon or Ashtaroth! And these Magians! They are really no more descendants of the priests in the Aryan home than I am a Greek. Half of them are nearly black—they are Hindus and speak Persian with an accent. They believe in a vast number of gods of all sizes and descriptions, and they sing hymns, in which they say that all these gods are the same. It is most confusing, and as the principal part of their chief sacrifice consists in making themselves exceedingly drunk with the detestable milkweed juice of which they are so fond, the performance is disgusting. The Great King began by saying that if they wished to sacrifice to their deities, they might do so, provided no one could find them doing it; and if they wished to be drunk, they might be drunk when and where they pleased; but that if they did the two together, he would crucify every Magian in Persia. His argument was very amusing. He said that a man who is drunk naturally speaks the truth, whereas a man who sacrifices to false gods inevitably tells lies; wherefore a man who sacrifices to false gods when he is drunk, runs the risk of telling lies and speaking the truth at the same time, and is consequently a creature revolting to logic, and must be immediately destroyed for the good of the whole race of mankind."

Nehushta had listened with varying attention to the

queen's account of the religious difficulties in the kingdom, and she laughed at the Megœric puzzle by which
Darius justified the death of the Magians.   But in her
heart she longed to see Zoroaster, and was weary of
entertaining her royal guest.   By way of diversion she
clapped her hands, and ordered the slaves who came
at her summons to bring sweetmeats and sherbet of
crushed fruit and snow.

"Are you fond of hunting?" asked Atossa, delicately
taking a little piece of white fig-paste.

"I have never been allowed to hunt," answered
Nehushta.   "Besides, it must be very tiring."

"I delight in it—the fig-paste is not so good as it
used to be—there is a new confectioner.   Darius considered that the former one had religious convictions
involving the telling of lies—and this is the result!
We are fallen low indeed when we cannot eat a·
Magian's pastry!   I am passionately fond of hunting,
but it is far from here to the desert and the lions are
scarce.   Besides, the men who are fit for lion-hunting
are generally engaged in hunting their fellow-creatures."

"Does the Great King hunt?" inquired Nehushta,
languidly sipping her sherbet from a green jade goblet,
as she lay among her cushions, supporting herself upon
one elbow.

"Whenever he has leisure.   He will talk of nothing
else to you——"

"Surely," interrupted Nehushta, with an air of perfect innocence, "I shall not be so far honoured as
that the Great King should talk with me?"

Atossa raised her blue eyes and looked curiously at
the dark princess.   She knew nothing of what had
passed the night before, save that the king had seen
Nehushta for a few moments, but she knew his char-

acter well enough to imagine that his frank and, as
she thought, undignified manner might have struck
Nehushta even in that brief interview. The idea that
the princess was already deceiving her flashed across
her mind. She smiled more tenderly than ever, with
a little added air of sadness that gave her a wonderful
charm.

"Yes, the Great King is very gracious to the ladies
of the court," she said. "You are so beautiful and so
different from them all that he will certainly talk long
with you after the banquet this evening—when he has
drunk much wine." The last words were added with
a most especial sweetness of tone.

Nehushta's face flushed a little and she drank more
sherbet before she answered. Then, letting her soft
dark eyes rest, as though in admiration, upon the
queen's face, she spoke in a tone of gentle deprecation :

> "*Shall a man prefer the darkness of night to the glories*
> *of risen day ?*
> *Or shall a man turn from the lilies to pluck the lowly*
> *flower of the field ?*"

"You know our poets, too?" exclaimed Atossa,
pleased with the graceful tone of the compliment, but
still looking at Nehushta with curious eyes. There
was a self-possession about the Hebrew princess that
she did not like ; it was as though some one had suddenly taken a quality of her own and made it theirs
and displayed it before her eyes. There was indeed
this difference, that while Atossa's calm and undisturbed
manner was generally real, Nehushta's was assumed,
and she herself felt that, at any moment, it might
desert her at her utmost need.

"So you know our poets?" repeated the queen, and

this time she laughed lightly. "Indeed I fear the king will talk to you more than ever, for he loves poetry. I daresay Zoroaster, too, has repeated many verses to you in the winter evenings at Ecbatana. He used to know endless poetry when he was a boy."

This time Nehushta looked at the queen, and wondered how she, who could not be more than two or three and twenty years old, although now married to her third husband, could speak of having known Zoroaster as a boy, seeing that he was past thirty years of age. She turned the question upon the queen.

"You must have seen Zoroaster very often before he left Shushan," she said. "You know him so well."

"Yes—every one knew him. He was the favourite of the court, with his beauty and his courage and his strange affection for that old—for the old Hebrew prophet. That is why Cambyses sent them both away," added she with a light laugh. "They were far too good, both of them, to be endured among the doings of those times."

Atossa spoke readily enough of Cambyses. Nehushta wondered whether she could be induced to speak of Smerdis. Her supposed ignorance of the true nature of what had occurred in the last few months would permit her to speak of the dead usurper with impunity.

"I suppose there have been great changes lately in the manners of the court — during this last year," suggested Nehushta carelessly. She pulled a raisin from the dry stem, and tried to peel it with her delicate fingers.

"Indeed there have been changes," answered Atossa, calmly. "A great many things that used to be tolerated will never be heard of now. On the whole, the change has been rather in relation to religion than otherwise. You will understand that in one year we have had three court religions. Cambyses sacrificed to Ashtaroth—and I must say he made a most appropriate choice of his tutelary goddess. Smerdis"—continued the queen in measured tones and with the utmost calmness of manner—"Smerdis devoted himself wholly to the worship of Indra, who appeared to be a convenient association of all the most agreeable gods; and the Great King now rules the earth by the grace of Auramazda. I, for my part, have always inclined to the Hebrew conception of one God—perhaps that is much the same as Auramazda, the All-Wise. What do you think?"

Nehushta smiled at the deft way in which the queen avoided speaking of Smerdis by turning the conversation again to religious topics. But fearing another lecture on the comparative merits of idolatry, human sacrifice, and monotheism, she manifested very little interest in the subject.

"I daresay it is the same. Zoroaster always says so, and that was the one point that Daniel could never forgive him. The sun is coming through those plants upon your head—shall we not have our cushions moved into the shade at the other end?" She clapped her hands and rose languidly, offering her hand to Atossa. But the queen sprang lightly to her feet.

"I have stayed too long," she said. "Come with me, dearest princess, and we will go out into the orange gardens upon the upper terrace. Perhaps," she added, adjusting the folds of her mantle, "we shall find Zoroaster there, or some of the princes, or even the Great King himself. Or, perhaps, it would amuse you to see where I live?"

Nehushta received her mantle from her slaves, and one of them brought her a linen tiara in place of the gauze veil she had twisted about her hair. But Atossa would not permit the change.

"It is too beautiful!" she cried enthusiastically. "So new! you must really not change it."

She put her arm around Nehushta affectionately and led her towards the door of the inner staircase. Then suddenly she paused, as though recollecting herself.

"No," she said, "I will show you the way I came. It is shorter and you should know it. It may be of use to you."

So they left the balcony by the little door that was almost masked by one of the great pillars, and descended the dark stairs. Nehushta detested every sort of bodily inconvenience, and inwardly wished the queen had not changed her mind, but had led her by an easier way.

"It is not far," said the queen, descending rapidly in front of her.

"It is dreadfully steep," objected Nehushta, "and I can hardly see my way at all. How many steps are there?"

"Only a score more," answered the queen's voice, farther down. She seemed to be hurrying, but Nehushta had no intention of going any faster, and carefully groped her way. As she began to see a glimmer of light at the last turn of the winding stair, she heard loud voices in the corridor below. With the cautious instinct of her race, she paused and listened. The hard, quick tones of an angry man dominated the rest.

H

CHAPTER VIII.

ZOROASTER had sat for nearly an hour, his eyes fixed
on the blue sky, his thoughts wandering in contemplation of things greater and higher than those of earth,
when he was roused by the measured tread of armed
men marching in a distant room. In an instant he stood
up, his helmet on his head,—the whole force of military habit bringing him back suddenly to the world of
reality. In a moment the same heavy curtain, from
under which Atossa had issued two hours before, was
drawn aside, and a double file of spearmen came out
upon the balcony, ranging themselves to right and left
with well-drilled precision. A moment more, and the
king himself appeared, walking alone, in his armour
and winged helmet, his left hand upon the hilt of his
sword, his splendid mantle hanging to the ground behind his shoulders. As he came between the soldiers,
he walked more slowly, and his dark, deep-set eyes
seemed to scan the bearing and accoutrements of each
separate spearman. It was rarely indeed, in those
early days of his power, that he laid aside his breastplate for the tunic, or his helmet for the tiara and
royal crown. In his whole air and gait the character of the soldier dominated, and the look of the
conqueror was already in his face.

Zoroaster strode forward a few paces, and stood

still as the king caught sight of him, preparing to prostrate himself, according to the ancient custom. But Darius checked him by a gesture; turning half round, he dismissed the guard, who filed back through the door as they had come, and the curtain fell behind them.

"I like not these elaborate customs," said the king. "A simple salutation, the hand to the lips and forehead—it is quite enough. A man might win a battle if he had all the time that it takes him to fall down at my feet and rise up again, twenty times in a day."

As the king's speech seemed to require no answer, Zoroaster stood silently waiting for his orders. Darius walked to the balustrade and stood in the full glare of the sun for a moment, looking out. Then he came back again.

"The town seems to be quiet this morning," he said. "How long did the queen tarry here talking with thee, Zoroaster?"

"The queen talked with her servant for the space of half an hour," answered Zoroaster, without hesitation, though he was astonished at the suddenness and directness of the question.

"She is gone to see thy princess," continued the king.

"The queen told her servant it was yet too early to see Nehushta," remarked the warrior.

"She is gone to see her, nevertheless," asserted Darius, in a tone of conviction. "Now, it stands in reason that when the most beautiful woman in the world has been told that another woman is come who is more beautiful than she, she will not lose a moment in seeing her." He eyed Zoroaster curiously for a moment, and his thick black beard did not altogether hide the smile on his face. "Come," he added, "we shall find the two together."

The king led the way and Zoroaster gravely followed. They passed down the staircase by which the queen had gone, and entering the low passage, came to the small door which she had bolted behind her with so much difficulty. The king pushed his weight against it, but it was still fastened.

"Thou art stronger than I, Zoroaster," he said, with a deep laugh. "Open this door."

The young warrior pushed heavily against the planks, and felt that one of them yielded. Then, standing back, he dealt a heavy blow on the spot with his clenched fist; a second, and the plank broke in. He put his arm through the aperture, and easily slipped the bolt back, and the door flew open. The blood streamed from his hand.

"That is well done," said Darius as he entered. His quick eye saw something white upon the stone bench in the dusky corner by the door. He stooped and picked it up quickly. It was the sealed scroll Atossa had left there when she needed both her hands to draw the bolt. Darius took it to one of the narrow windows, looked at it curiously and broke the seal. Zoroaster stood near and wiped the blood from his bruised knuckle.

The contents of the scroll were short. It was addressed to one Phraortes, of Ecbatana in Media, and contained the information that the Great King had returned in triumph from Babylon, having subdued the rebels and slain many thousands in two battles. Furthermore, that the said Phraortes should give instant information of the queen's affairs, and do nothing in regard to them until further intimation arrived.

The king stood a moment in deep thought. Then he walked slowly down the corridor, holding the scroll loose in his hand. Just at that instant Atossa emerged from the dark staircase, and as she found herself face to face with Darius, she uttered an exclamation and stood still.

"This is a very convenient place for our interview," said Darius quietly. "No one can hear us. Therefore speak the truth at once." He held up the scroll to her eyes.

Atossa's ready wit did not desert her, nor did she change colour, though she knew her life was in the balance with her words. She laughed lightly as she spoke:

"I came down the stairs this morning———"

"To see the most beautiful woman in the world," interrupted Darius, raising his voice. . "You have seen her. I am glad of it. Why did you bolt the door of the passage?"

"Because I thought it unfitting that the passage to the women's apartments should be left open when so many in the palace know the way," she answered readily enough.

"Where were you taking this letter when you left it at the door?" asked the king, beginning to doubt whether there were anything wrong after all.

"I was about to send it to Ecbatana," answered Atossa with perfect simplicity.

"Who is this Phraortes?"

"He is the governor of the lands my father gave me for my own in Media. I wrote him to tell him of the Great King's victory, and that he should send me information concerning my affairs, and do nothing further until he hears from me."

" Why not ?"

" Because I thought it possible that the Great King would spend the summer in Ecbatana, and that I should therefore be there myself to give my own directions. I· forgot the letter because I had to take both hands to draw the bolt, and I was coming back to get it. Nehushta the princess is with me—she is now upon the staircase."

The king looked thoughtfully at his wife's beautiful face.

" You have evidently spoken the truth," he said slowly. " But it is not always easy to understand what your truth signifies. I often think it would be much wiser to strangle you. Say you that Nehushta is near ? Call her, then. Why does she tarry ?"

In truth Nehushta had trembled as she crouched upon the stairs, not knowing whether to descend or to fly up the steps again. As she heard the queen pronounce her name, however, she judged it prudent to seem to have been out of earshot, and with quick, soft steps, she went up till she came to the lighted part, and there she waited.

" Let the Great King go himself and find her," said Atossa proudly, " if he doubts me any further." She stood aside to let him pass. But Darius beckoned to Zoroaster to go. He had remained standing at some distance, an unwilling witness to the royal altercation that had taken place before him ; but as he passed the queen, she gave him a glance of imploring sadness, as though beseeching his sympathy in what she was made to suffer. He ran quickly up the steps in spite of the darkness, and found Nehushta waiting by the window higher up. She started as he appeared, for he was the person she least expected. But he took her quickly in his arms, and kissed her passionately twice.

"Come quickly, my beloved," he whispered. "The king waits below."

"I heard his voice—and then I fled," she whispered hurriedly; and they began to descend again. "I hate her—I knew I should," she whispered, as she leaned upon his arm. So they emerged into the corridor, and met Darius waiting for them. The queen was nowhere to be seen, and the door at the farther extremity of the narrow way was wide open.

The king was as calm as though nothing had occurred; he still held the open letter in his hand as Nehushta entered the passage, and bowed herself before him. He took her hand for a moment, and then dropped it; but his eyes flashed suddenly and his arm trembled at her touch.

"Thou hadst almost lost thy way," he said. "The palace is large and the passages are many and devious. Come now, I will lead thee to the gardens. There thou canst find friends among the queen's noble women, and amusements of many kinds. Let thy heart delight in the beauty of Shushan, and if there is anything that thou desirest, ask and I will give it thee."

Nehushta bent her head in thanks. The only thing she desired was to be alone for half an hour with Zoroaster; and that seemed difficult.

"Thy servant desireth what is pleasant in thy sight," she answered. And so they left the passage by the open door, and the king himself conducted Nehushta to the entrance of the garden, and bade the slave-woman who met them to lead her to the pavilion where the ladies of the palace spent the day in the

warm summer weather.   Zoroaster knew that whatever liberty his singular position allowed him in the
quarter of the building where the king himself lived,
he was not privileged to enter that place which was
set apart for the noble ladies. Darius hated to be always
surrounded by guards and slaves, and the terraces and
staircases of his dwelling were generally totally deserted,
—only small detachments of spearmen guarding jealously
the main entrances.   But the remainder of the palace
swarmed with the gorgeously dressed retinue of the
court, with slaves of every colour and degree, from the
mute smooth-faced Ethiopian to the accomplished
Hebrew scribes of the great nobles ; from the black
and scantily-clad fan-girls to the dainty Greek tirewomen of the queen's toilet, who loitered near the
carved marble fountain at the entrance to the gardens ;
and in the outer courts, detachments of the horsemen
of the guard rubbed their weapons, or reddened their
broad leather bridles and trappings with red chalk, or
groomed the horse of some lately arrived officer or
messenger, or hung about and basked in the sun, with
no clothing but their short-sleeved linen tunics and
breeches, discussing the affairs of the nation with the
certainty of decision peculiar to all soldiers, high and
low.   There was only room for a squadron of horse in
the palace ; but though they were few, they were the
picked men of the guard, and every one of them felt
himself as justly entitled to an opinion concerning the
position of the new king, as though he were at least a
general.

    But Darius allowed no gossiping slaves nor wran-
gling soldiers in his own dwelling.   There all was
silent and apparently deserted, and thither he led
Zoroaster again.   The young warrior was astonished

at the way in which the king moved about unattended, as carelessly as though he were a mere soldier himself; he was not yet accustomed to the restless independence of character, to the unceasing activity and perfect personal fearlessness of the young Darius. It was hard to realise that this simple, hard-handed, outspoken man was the Great King, and occupied the throne of the magnificent and stately Cyrus, who never stirred abroad without the full state of the court about him; or that he reigned in the stead of the luxurious Cambyses, who feared to tread upon uncovered marble, or to expose himself to the draught of a staircase; and who, after seven years of caring for his body, had destroyed himself in a fit of impotent passion. Darius succeeded to the throne of Persia as a lion coming into the place of jackals, as an eagle into a nest of crows and carrion birds—untiring, violent, relentless and brave.

"Knowest thou one Phraortes, of Ecbatana?" the king asked suddenly when he was alone with Zoroaster.

"I know him," answered the prince. "A man rich and powerful, full of vanity as a peacock, and of wiles like a serpent. Not noble. He is the son of a fish-vendor, grown rich by selling salted sturgeons in the market-place. He is also the overseer of the queen's farmlands in Media, and of the Great King's horse-breeding stables."

"Go forth and bring him to me," said the king shortly. Without a word, Zoroaster made a brief salute and turned upon his heel to go. But it was as though a man had thrust him through with a knife. The king gazed after him in admiration of his magnificent obedience.

"Stay!" he called out. "How long wilt thou be gone?"

Zoroaster turned sharply round in military fashion, as he answered:

"It is a hundred and fifty farsangs [1] to Ecbatana. By the king's relays I can ride there in six days, and I can bring back Phraortes in six days more—if he die not of the riding," he added, with a grim smile.

"Is he old, or young? Fat, or meagre?" asked the king, laughing.

"He is a man of forty years, neither thin nor fat —a good horseman in his way, but not as we are."

"Bind him to his horse if he falls off from weariness. And tell him he is summoned to appear before me. Tell him the business brooks no delay. Auramazda be with thee and bring thee help. Go with speed."

Again Zoroaster turned and in a moment he was gone. He had sworn to be the king's faithful servant, and he would keep his oath, cost what it might, though it was bitterness to him to leave Nehushta without a word. He bethought him as he hastily put on light garments for the journey, that he might send her a letter, and he wrote a few words upon a piece of parchment, and folded it together. As he passed by the entrance of the garden on his way to the stables, he looked about for one of Nehushta's slaves; but seeing none, he beckoned to one of the Greek tirewomen, and giving her a piece of gold, bade her take the little scroll to Nehushta, the Hebrew princess, who was in the gardens. Then he went quickly on, and mounting the best horse in the king's stables, galloped at a break-neck pace down the steep incline. In five minutes he had crossed the bridge, and was speeding

[1] Between five and six hundred English miles. South American postilions at the present day ride six hundred miles a week for a bare living.

over the straight, dusty road toward Nineveh. In a quarter of an hour, a person watching him from the palace would have seen his flying figure disappearing as in a tiny speck of dust far out upon the broad, green plain.

But the Greek slave-woman stood with Zoroaster's letter in her hand and held the gold piece he had given her in her mouth, debating what she should do. She was one of the queen's women, as it chanced, and she immediately reflected that she might turn the writing to some better account than by delivering it to Nehushta, whom she had seen for a moment that morning as she passed, and whose dark Hebrew face displeased the frivolous Greek, for some hidden reason. She thought of giving the scroll to the queen, but then she reflected that she did not know what it contained. The words were written hastily and in the Chaldean character. Their import might displease her mistress. The woman was not a newcomer, and she knew Zoroaster's face well enough from former times; she knew also, or suspected, that the queen secretly loved him, and she argued from the fact of Zoroaster, who was dressed for a journey, sending so hastily a word to Nehushta, that he loved the Hebrew princess. Therefore, if the letter were a mere love greeting, with no name written in it, the queen might apply it to herself, and she would be pleased; whereas, if it were in any way clear that the writing was intended for Nehushta, the queen would certainly be glad that it should never be delivered. The result of this cunning argument was that the Greek woman thrust the letter into her bosom, and the gold piece into her girdle; and went to seek an opportunity of seeing the queen alone.

That day, towards evening, Atossa sat in an inner
chamber before her great mirror; the table was covered
with jade boxes, silver combs, bowls of golden hair-
pins, little ivory instruments, and all the appurtenances
of her toilet. Two or three magnificent jewels lay
among the many articles of use, gleaming in the
reflected light of the two tall lamps that stood on
bronze stands beside her chair. She was fully attired
and had dismissed her women; but she lingered a
moment, poring over the little parchment scroll her
chief hairdresser had slipped into her hand when they
were alone for a moment. Only a black fan-girl stood
a few paces behind her, and resting the stem of the
long palm against one foot thrust forward, swung the
broad round leaf quickly from side to side at arm's
length, sending a constant stream of fresh air upon her
royal mistress, just below the level of the lamps which
burned steadily above.

The queen turned the small letter again in her
hand, and smiled to herself as she looked into the
great burnished sheet of silver that surmounted the
table. With some difficulty she had mastered the
contents, for she knew enough of Hebrew and of the
Chaldean character to comprehend the few simple
words.

"I go hence for twelve days upon the king's
business. My beloved, my soul is with thy soul and
my heart with thy heart. As the dove that goeth
forth in the morning and returneth in the evening to
his mate, so I will return soon to thee."

Atossa knew well enough that the letter had been
intended for Nehushta. The woman had whispered
that Zoroaster had given it to her, and Zoroaster would
never have written those words to herself; or, writing

anything, would not have written in the Hebrew language.

But as the queen read, her heart rose up in wrath against the Persian prince and against the woman he loved. When she had talked with him that morning, she had felt her old yearning affection rising again in her breast. She had wondered at herself, being accustomed to think that she was beyond all feeling for man, and the impression she had received from her half-hour's talk with him was so strong, that she had foolishly delayed sending her letter to Phraortes, in order to see the woman Zoroaster admired, and had, in her absence of mind, forgotten the scroll upon the seat in the corridor, and had brought herself into such desperate danger through the discovery of the missive, that she hardly yet felt safe. The king had dismissed her peremptorily from his presence while he waited for Nehushta, and she had not seen him during the rest of the day. As for Zoroaster, she had soon heard from her women that he had taken the road towards Nineveh before noon, alone and almost unarmed, mounted upon one of the fleetest horses in Persia. She had not a doubt that Darius had despatched him at once to Ecbatana to meet Phraortes, or at least to inquire into the state of affairs in the city. She knew that no one could outride Zoroaster, and that there was nothing to be done but to await the issue. It was not possible to send a word of warning to her agent—he must inevitably take his chance, and if his conduct attracted suspicion, he would, in all probability, be at once put to death. She believed that, even in that event, she could easily clear herself; but she resolved, if possible, to warn him as soon as he reached Shushan, or even to induce the king to be absent from the palace for a few

days at the time when Phraortes might be expected.
There was plenty of time—at least eleven days.

Meanwhile, a desperate struggle was beginning
within her, and the letter her woman had brought her
hastened the conclusion to which her thoughts were
rapidly tending.

She felt keenly the fact that Zoroaster, who had been
so cold to her advances in former days, had preferred
before her a Hebrew woman, and was now actually so
deeply in love with Nehushta, that he could not leave
the palace for a few days without writing her a word
of love—he, who had never loved any one! She
fiercely hated this dark woman, who was preferred
before her by the man she secretly loved, and whom
the king had brutally declared to be the most beautiful
woman in the world. She longed for her destruction
as she had never longed for anything in her life. Her
whole soul rose in bitter resentment; not only did
Zoroaster love this black-eyed, dark-browed child of
captivity, but the king, who had always maintained
that Atossa was unequalled in the world, even when
he coldly informed her that he would never trust her,
now dared to say before Zoroaster, almost before
Nehushta herself, that the princess was the more beautiful of the two. The one man wounded her in her
vanity, the other in her heart.

It would not be possible at present to be revenged
upon the king. There was little chance of eluding his
sleepless vigilance, or of leading him into any rash act
of self-destruction. Besides, she knew him too well
not to understand that he was the only man alive who
could save Persia from further revolutions, and keep
the throne against all comers. She loved power and
the splendour of her royal existence, perhaps more than

she loved Zoroaster. The idea of another change in the monarchy was not to be thought of, now that Darius had subdued Babylon. She had indeed a half-concerted plan with Phraortes to seize the power in Media in case the king were defeated in Babylonia, and the scroll she had so imprudently forgotten that very morning was merely an order to lay aside all such plans for the present, since the king had returned in triumph.

As far as her conscience was concerned, Atossa would as soon have overthrown and murdered the king to gratify the personal anger she felt against him at the present moment, as she would have wrecked the universe to possess a jewel she fancied. There existed in her mind no idea of proportion between the gratification of her passions and the means she might employ thereto; provided one gratification did not interfere with another which she always saw beyond. Nothing startled her on account of its mere magnitude; no plan was rejected by her merely because it implied ruin to a countless number of human beings who were useless to her. She coldly calculated the amount of satisfaction she could at any time obtain for her wishes and desires, so as not to prejudice the gratification of all the possible passions she might hereafter experience.

As for injuring Zoroaster, she would not have thought of it. She loved him in a way peculiar to herself, but it was love, nevertheless,—and she had no idea of wreaking her disappointment upon the object on which she had set her heart. As a logical consequence, she determined to turn all her anger against Nehushta, and she pictured to herself the delicious pleasure of torturing the young princess's jealousy to desperation.

To convince Nehushta that Zoroaster was deceiving
her, and really loved herself, the queen; to force
Zoroaster into some position where he must either
silently let Nehushta believe that he was attached to
Atossa, or, as an alternative, betray the king's secrets
by speaking the truth; to let Nehushta's vanity be
flattered by the king's admiration,—nay, even to force
her into a marriage with Darius, and then by suffering
her again to fall into her first love for Zoroaster, bring
her to a public disgrace by suddenly unmasking her
to the king—to accomplish these things surely and
quickly, reserving for herself the final delight of scoffing at her worsted rival—all this seemed to Atossa to
constitute a plan at once worthy of her profound and
scheming intelligence, and most sweetly satisfactory to
her injured vanity and rejected love.

It would be hard for her to see Nehushta married
to the king, and occupying the position of chief favourite
even for a time. But the triumph would be the sweeter
when Nehushta was finally overthrown, and meanwhile
there would be much daily delight in tormenting the
princess's jealousy. Chance, or rather the cunning of
her Greek tirewoman, had thrown a weapon in her
way which could easily be turned into an instrument
of torture, and as she sat before her mirror, she twisted
and untwisted the little bit of parchment, and smiled
to herself, a sweet bright smile—and leaned her head
back to the pleasant breeze of the fan.

CHAPTER IX.

THE noonday air was hot and dry in the garden of the palace, but in the graceful marble pavilion there was coolness and the sound of gently plashing water. Rose-trees and climbing plants screened the sunlight from the long windows, and gave a soft green tinge to the eight-sided hall, where a fountain played in the midst, its little jet falling into a basin hollowed in the floor. On the rippling surface a few water-lilies swayed gently with the constant motion, anchored by their long stems to the bottom. All was cool and quiet and restful, and Nehushta stood looking at the fountain.

She was alone and very unhappy. Zoroaster had left the palace without a word to her, and she knew only by the vague reports her slaves brought her, that he was gone for many days. Her heart sank at the thought of all that might happen before he returned, and the tears stood in her eyes.

"Are you here alone, dear princess?" said a soft, clear voice behind her. Nehushta started, as though something had stung her, as she recognised Atossa's tones. There was nothing of her assumed cordiality of the previous day as she answered. She was too unhappy, too weary of the thought that her lover was gone, to be able to act a part, or pretend a friendliness she did not feel.

" Yes—I am alone," she said quietly.

" So am I," answered Atossa, her blue eyes sparkling
with the sunshine she brought in with her, and all her
wonderful beauty beaming, as it were, with an overflowing happiness.   " The ladies of the court are gone
in state to the city, in the Great King's train, and you
and I are alone in the palace.   How deliciously cool
it is in here."

She sat down upon a heap of cushions by one of the
·screened windows and contemplated Nehushta, who
still stood by the fountain.

" You look sad—and tired, dearest Nehushta," said
she presently.   " Indeed you must not be sad here—
nobody is sad here ! "

" I am sad," repeated Nehushta, in a dreary, monotonous way, as though scarcely conscious of what she
was saying.   There was a moment's silence before
Atossa spoke again.

" Tell me what it is," she said at last, in persuasive
accents.   " Tell me what is the matter.   It may be that
you lack something—that you miss something you were
, used to in Ecbatana.   Will you not tell me, dearest ? "

" Tell you what ? " asked Nehushta, as though she
had not heard.

" Tell me what it is that makes you sad," repeated
the queen.

" Tell you ? " exclaimed the princess, suddenly looking up, with flashing eyes, " tell *you?* oh no ! "

Atossa looked a little sadly at Nehushta, as though
hurt at the want of confidence she showed.   But the
Hebrew maiden turned away and went and looked
through the hanging plants at the garden without.
Then Atossa rose softly and came and stood behind
her, and put her arm about her, and let her own fair

cheek rest against the princess's dark face. Nehushta said nothing, but she trembled, as though something she hated were touching her.

"Is it because your friend has gone away suddenly?" asked Atossa almost in a whisper, with the sweetest accent of sympathy. Nehushta started a little.

"No!" she answered, almost fiercely. "Why do you say that?"

"Only—he wrote me a little word before he went. I thought you might like to know he was safe," replied the queen, gently pressing her arm about Nehushta's slender waist.

"Wrote to you?" repeated the princess, in angry surprise.

"Yes, dearest," answered the queen, looking down in well-feigned embarrassment. "I would not have told you, only I thought you would wish to hear of him. If you like, I will read you a part of what he says," she added, producing from her bosom the little piece of parchment carefully rolled together.

It was more than Nehushta could bear. Her olive skin turned suddenly pale, and she tore herself away from the queen.

"Oh no! no! I will not hear it! Leave me in peace—for your gods' sake, leave me in peace!"

Atossa drew herself up and stared coldly at Nehushta, as though she were surprised beyond measure and deeply offended.

"Truly, I need not to be told twice to leave you in peace," she said proudly. "I thought to comfort you, because I saw you were sad—even at the expense of my own feelings. I will leave you now—but I bear no malice against you. You are very, very young, and very, very foolish."

Atossa shook her head, thoughtfully, and swept from
the pavilion in stately and offended dignity. But as
she walked alone through the garden, she smiled to herself and softly hummed a merry melody she had heard
from an Egyptian actor on the previous evening.
Darius had brought a company of Egyptians from
Babylon, and after the banquet, had commanded that
they should perform their music, and dancing, and
mimicry, for the amusement of the assembled court.

Atossa's sweet voice echoed faintly among the orange
trees and the roses, as she went towards the palace,
and the sound of it came distantly to Nehushta's ears.
She stood for a while where the queen had left her,
her face pale and her hands wringing together; and
then, with a sudden impulse, she went and threw herself upon the floor, and buried her head in the deep,
soft cushions. Her hands wandered in the wealth of
her black hair, and her quick, hot tears stained the
delicate silk of the pillows.

How could he? How was it possible? He said he
loved her, and now, when he was sent away for many
days, his only thought had been to write to the queen
—not to herself! An agony of jealousy overwhelmed
her, and she could have torn out her very soul, and
trampled her own heart under her feet in her anger.
Passionately she clasped her hands to her temples;
her head seemed splitting with a new and dreadful pain
that swallowed all her thoughts for a moment, until the
cold weight seemed again to fall upon her breast and all
her passion gushed out in abundant tears. Suddenly
a thought struck her. She roused herself, leaning upon
one hand, and stared vacantly a moment at her small
gilded shoe which had fallen from her bare foot upon
the marble pavement. She absently reached forward

and took the thing in her hand, and gravely contemplated the delicate embroidery and thick gilding, through her tears,—as one will do a foolish and meaningless thing in the midst of a great sorrow.

Was it possible that the queen had deceived her? How she wished she had let her read the writing as she had offered to do. She did not imagine at first that the letter was for herself and had gone astray. But she thought the queen might easily have pretended to have received something, or had even scratched a few words upon a bit of parchment, meaning to pass it off upon her as a letter from Zoroaster. She longed to possess the thing and to judge of it with her own eyes. It would hardly be possible to say whether it were written by him or not, as far as the handwriting was concerned; but Nehushta was sure she should recognise some word, some turn of language that would assure her that it was his. She could almost have risen and gone in search of the queen at once, to prove the lie upon her—to challenge her to show the writing. But her pride forbade her. She had been so weak— she should not have let Atossa see, even for a moment, that she was hurt, not even that she loved Zoroaster. She had tried to conceal her feelings, but Atossa had gone too far, had tortured her beyond all endurance, and she knew that, even if she had known what to expect, she could not have easily borne the soft, infuriating, deadly, caressing, goading taunts of that fair, cruel woman.

Then again, the whole possibility of Zoroaster's unfaithfulness came and took shape before her. He had known and loved Atossa of old, perhaps, and now the old love had risen up and killed the new—he had sworn so truly under the ivory moonlight in Ecbatana.

And yet—he had written to this other woman and not to her. Was it true? Was it Atossa's cruel lie? In a storm of doubt and furious passion, her tears welled forth again; and once more she hid her face in the pale yellow cushions, and her whole beautiful body trembled and was wrung with her sobs.

Suddenly she was aware that some one entered the little hall and stood beside her. She dared not look up at first; she was unstrung and wretched in her grief and anger, and it was the strong, firm tread of a man. The footsteps ceased, and the intruder, whoever he might be, was standing still; she took courage and looked quickly up. It was the king himself. Indeed, she might have known that no other man would dare to penetrate into the recesses of the garden set apart for the ladies of the palace.

Darius stood quietly gazing at her with an expression of doubt and curiosity, that was almost amusing, on his stern, dark face. Nehushta was frightened, and sprang to her feet with the graceful quickness of a startled deer. She was indolent by nature, but as swift as light when she was roused by fear or excitement.

"Are you so unhappy in my palace?" asked Darius gently. "Why are you weeping? Who has hurt you?"

Nehushta turned her face away and dashed the tears from her eyes, while her cheeks flushed hotly.

"I am not weeping—no one—has hurt me," she answered, in a voice broken rather by embarrassment and annoyance, than by the sorrow she had nearly forgotten in her sudden astonishment at being face to face with the king.

Darius smiled, and almost laughed, as he stroked his thick beard with his broad brown hand.

"Princess," he said, "will you sit down again? I will deliver you a discourse upon the extreme folly of ever telling"—he hesitated—"of saying anything which is not precisely true."

There was something so simple and honest in his manner of speaking, that Nehushta almost smiled through her half-dried tears as she sat upon the cushions at the king's feet. He himself sat down upon the broad marble seat that ran round the eight-sided little building, and composing his face to a serious expression, that was more than half-assumed, began to deliver his lecture.

"I take it for granted that when one tells a lie, he expects to be believed. There must, then, be something or circumstance which can help to make his lies credible. Now, my dear princess, in the present instance, while I was looking you in the face and counting the tears upon your very beautiful cheeks, you deliberately told me that you were not weeping. There was, therefore, not even the shadow of a thing, or circumstance which could make what you said credible. It is evident that what you said was not true. Is it not so?"

Nehushta could not help smiling as she looked up and saw the kindly light in the king's dark eyes. She thought she understood he was amusing her for the sake of giving her time to collect herself, and in spite of the determined intention of marrying her he had so lately expressed, she felt safe with him.

"The king lives for ever," she answered, in the set phrase of assent common at the court.

"It is very probable," replied Darius gravely. "So many people say so, that I should have to believe all mankind liars if that were not true. But I must return to your own particular case. It would have been easy for you not to have said what you did. I must therefore suppose that in going out of the way to make an attempt to deceive me in the face of such evidence—by saying you were not weeping when the tears were actually falling from those very soft eyes of yours—you had an object to gain. Men employ truth and falsehood for much the same reason: A man who does not respect truth will, therefore, lie when he can hope to gain more by it. The man who lies expects to gain something by his lie, and the man who tells the truth hopes that, in so doing, he will establish himself a credit which he can use upon future occasions.[1] But the object is the same. Tell me, therefore, princess, what did you hope to gain by trying to deceive me?" Darius laughed as he concluded his argument and looked at Nehushta to see what she would say—Nehushta laughed also, she could hardly tell why. The king's brilliant, active humour was catching. She reached out and thrust her foot into the little slipper that still lay beside her, before she answered.

"What I said was true in one way and not in another," she said. "I had been crying bitterly, but I stopped when I heard the king come and stand beside me. So it was only the tears the king saw and not the weeping. As for the object,"—she laughed a little,—"it was, perhaps, that I might gain time to dry my eyes."

Darius shifted his position a little.

"I know," he said gravely. "And I know why you were weeping, and it is my fault. Will you forgive me, princess? I am a hasty man, not accustomed to think twice when I give my commands."

[1] Herodotus, book iii. chap. lxxii.

Nehushta looked up suddenly with an expression of inquiry.

"I sent him away very quickly," continued the king. "If I had thought, I would have told him to come and bid you farewell. He would not have willingly gone without seeing you—it was my fault. He will return in twelve days."

Nehushta was silent and bit her lip as the bitter thought arose in her heart that it was not alone Zoroaster's sudden departure that had pained her. Then it floated across her mind that the king had purposely sent away her lover in order that he might himself try to win her heart.

"Why did you send him—and not another?" she asked, without looking up, and forgetting all formality of speech.

"Because he is the man of all others whom I can trust, and I needed a faithful messenger," answered Darius, simply.

Nehushta gazed into the king's face searching for some sign there, but he had spoken earnestly enough.

"I thought——" she began, and then stopped short, blushing crimson.

"You thought," answered Darius, "that I had sent him away never to return because I desire you for my wife. It was natural, but it was unjust. I sent him because I was obliged to do so. If you wish it, I will leave you now, and I will promise you that I will not look upon your face till Zoroaster returns."

Nehushta looked down and she still blushed. She could hardly believe her ears.

"Indeed," she faltered, "it were perhaps—best—I mean——" she could not finish the sentence. Darius rose quietly from his seat:

"Farewell, princess; it shall be as you desire," he said gravely, and strode towards the door. His face was pale and his lips set tight.

Nehushta hesitated and then, in a moment, she comprehended the whole nobility of soul of the young king,—a man at whose words the whole land trembled, who crushed his enemies like empty egg-shells beneath his feet, and yet who, when he held the woman he loved completely in his power, refused, even for a moment, to intrude his presence upon her against her wish.

She sprang from her seat and ran to him, and kneeled on one knee and took his hand. He did not look at her, but his own hand trembled violently in hers, and he made as though he would lift her to her feet.

"Nay," she cried, "let not my lord be angry with his handmaiden! Let the king grant me my request, for he is the king of men and of kings!" In her sudden emotion she spoke once more in the form of a humble subject addressing her sovereign.

"Speak, princess," answered Darius. "If it be possible, I will grant your request."

"I would——" she stopped, and again the generous blood overspread her dark cheek. "I would—I know not what I would, saving to thank thee for thy goodness and kindness—I was unhappy, and thou hast comforted me. I meant not that it was best that I should not look upon the king's face." She spoke the last words in so low a tone as she bent her head, that Darius could scarcely hear them. But his willing ears interpreted rightly what she said, and he understood.

"Shall I come to you to-morrow, princess, at the same hour?" he asked, almost humbly.

"Nay, the king knoweth that the garden is ever full of the women of the court," said Nehushta, hesitating; for she thought that it would be a very different matter to be seen from a distance by all the ladies of the palace in conversation with the king.

"Do not fear," answered Darius. "The garden shall be yours. There are other bowers of roses in Shushan whither the women can go. None but you shall enter here, so long as it be your pleasure. Farewell, I will come to you to-morrow at noon."

He turned and looked into her eyes, and then she took his hand and silently placed it upon her forehead in thanks. In a moment he was gone and she could hear his quick tread upon the marble of the steps outside, and in the path through the roses. When she knew that he was out of sight, Nehushta went out and stood in the broad blaze of the noonday sun. She passed her hand over her forehead, as though she had been dazed. It seemed as though a change had come over her and she could not understand it.

In the glad security of being alone, she ran swiftly down one of the paths, and across by another. Then she stopped short and bent down a great bough of blooming roses and buried her beautiful dark face in the sweet leaves and smelled the perfume, and laughed.

"Oh! I am so happy!" she cried aloud. But her face suddenly became grave, as she tried to understand what she felt. After all, Zoroaster was only gone for twelve days, and meanwhile she had secured her liberty, the freedom of wandering all day in the beautiful gardens, and she could dream of him to her heart's content. And the letter? It was a forgery, of course. That wicked queen loved Zoroaster and wished to make Nehushta give him up! Perhaps she might tell the

king something of it when he came on the next day.
He would be so royally angry! He would so hate the
lie! And yet, in some way, it seemed to her that she
could not tell Darius of this trouble. He had been so
kind, so gentle, as though he had been her brother,
instead of the Great King himself, who bore life and
death in his right hand and his left, whose shadow was
a terror to the world already, and at whose brief, imperious word a nation rose to arms and victory. Was
this the terrible Darius? The man who had slain the
impostor with his own sword? who had vanquished
rebel Babylon in a few days and brought home four
thousand captives at his back? He was as gentle as
a girl, this savage warrior—but when she recalled his
features, she remembered the stern look that came into
his face when he was serious, she grew thoughtful and
wandered slowly down the path, biting a rose-leaf
delicately with her small white teeth and thinking
many things; most of all, how she might be revenged upon Atossa for what she had suffered that
morning.

But Atossa herself was enjoying at that very moment
the triumph of the morning and quietly planning how
she might continue the torment she had imagined for
Nehushta, without allowing its cruelty to diminish,
while keeping herself amused and occupied to the
fullest extent until Zoroaster should return. It was
not long before she learned from her chief tirewoman
that the king had been in the pavilion of the garden
with Nehushta that morning, and it at once occurred
to her that, if the king returned on the following day,
it would be an easy thing to appear while he was with
the princess, and by veiled words and allusions to
Zoroaster, to make her rival suffer the most excruciating

torments, which she would be forced to conceal from the king.

But, at the same time, the news gave her cause for serious thought. · She had certainly not intended that Nehushta should be left alone for hours with Darius. She knew indeed that the princess loved Zoroaster, but she could not conceive that any woman should be insensible to the consolation the Great King could offer. If affairs took such a turn, she fully intended to allow the king to marry Nehushta, while she confidently believed it in her power to destroy her just when she had reached the summit of her ambition.

It chanced that the king chose that day to eat his evening meal in the sole company of Atossa, as he sometimes did when weary of the court ceremony. When, therefore, they reclined at sundown upon a small secluded terrace of the upper story, Atossa found an excellent opportunity of discussing Nehushta and her doings.

Darius lay upon a couch on one side of the low table, and Atossa was opposite to him. The air was dry and intensely hot, and on each side two black fan-girls plied their palm-leaves silently with all their might. The king lay back upon his cushions, his head uncovered, and all his shaggy curls of black hair tossed behind him, his broad, strong hand circling a plain goblet of gold that stood beside him on the table. For once, he had laid aside his breastplate, and a vest of white and purple fell loosely over his tunic; but his sword of keen Indian steel lay within reach upon the floor.

Atossa had raised herself upon her elbow, and her clear blue eyes were fixed upon the king's face, thoughtfully, as though expecting that he would say something. Contrary to all custom, she wore a Greek tunic with short sleeves caught at the shoulders by golden buckles, and her fair hair was gathered into a heavy knot, low down, behind her head. Her dazzling arms and throat were bare, but above her right elbow she wore a thick twisted snake of gold, her only ornament.

"The king is not athirst to-night," said Atossa at last, watching the full goblet that he grasped, but did not raise.

"I am not always thirsty," answered Darius moodily. "Would you have me always drunk, like a Babylonian dog?"

"No; nor always sober, like a Persian captain."

"What Persian captain?" asked the king, suddenly looking at her and knitting his brows.

"Why, like him, whom, for his sobriety you have sent to-day on the way to Nineveh," answered Atossa.

"I have sent no one to Nineveh to-day."

"To Ecbatana then, to inquire whether I told you the truth about my poor servant Phraortes—Fravartish, as you call him," said the queen, with a flash of spite in her blue eyes.

"I assure you," answered the king, laughing, "that it is solely on account of your remarkable beauty that I have not had you strangled. So soon as you grow ugly you shall surely die. It is very unwise of me, as it is!"

The queen, too, laughed, a low, silvery laugh.

"I am greatly indebted for my life," said she. "I am very beautiful, I am aware, but I am no longer the most beautiful woman in the world." She spoke without a trace of annoyance in her voice or face, as though it were a good jest.

"No," said Darius, thoughtfully. "I used to think that you were. It is in the nature of man to change his opinion. You are, nevertheless, very beautiful—I admire your Greek dress."

"Shall I send my tirewoman with one like it to Nehushta?" inquired Atossa, raising her delicate eyebrows, with a sweet smile.

"You will not need to improve her appearance in order that she may find favour in my eyes," answered Darius, laughing. "But the jest is good. You would rather send her an Indian snake than an ornament."

"Yes," returned the queen, who understood the king's strange character better than any one. "You cannot in honesty expect me not to hate a woman whom you think more beautiful than me! It would hardly be natural. It is unfortunate that she should prefer the sober Persian captain to the king himself."

"It is unfortunate—yes—fortunate for you, however."

"I mean, it will chafe sadly upon you when you have married her," said Atossa, calmly.

Darius raised the goblet he still held and setting it to his lips drank it at a draught. As he replaced it on the table, Atossa rose swiftly, and with her own hands refilled it from a golden ewer. The wine was of Shiraz, dark and sweet and strong. The king took her small white hand in his, as she stood beside him, and looked at it.

"It is a beautiful hand," he said. "Nehushta's fingers are a trifle shorter than yours—a little more pointed—a little less grasping. Shall I marry Nehushta, or not?" He looked up as he asked the question, and he laughed.

"No," answered Atossa, laughing too.

"Shall I marry her to Zoroaster?"

"No," she answered again, but her laugh was less natural.

"What shall I do with her?" asked the king.

"Strangle her!" replied Atossa, with a little fierce pressure on his hand as he held hers, and without the least hesitation.

"There would be frequent sudden deaths in Persia, if you were king," said Darius.

"It seems to me there are enough slain, as it is," answered the queen. "There are, perhaps, one—or two——"

Suddenly the king's face grew grave, and he dropped her hand.

"Look you!" he said, "I love jesting. But jest not overmuch with me. Do no harm to Nehushta, or I will make an end of your jesting for ever, by sure means. That white throat of yours would look ill with a bow-string about it."

The queen bit her lip. The king seldom spoke to her in earnest, and she was frightened.

On the following day, when she went to the garden, two tall spearmen guarded the entrance, and as she was about to go in, they crossed their lances over the marble door and silently barred the way.

CHAPTER X.

ATOSSA started back in pure astonishment and stared
for a moment at the two guards, looking from one to
the other, and trying to read their stolid faces.   Then
she laid her hand on their spears, and would have
pushed them aside ; but she could not.

"Whose hounds are ye ?" she said angrily.   "Know
ye not the queen ?   Make way !"

But the two strong soldiers neither answered nor
removed their weapons from before the door.

"Dog-faced slaves !" she said between her teeth.
"I will crucify you both before sundown !"   She
turned and went away, but she was glad that no one
was there in the narrow vestibule before the garden to
see her discomfiture.   It was the first time in her life
she had ever been resisted by an inferior, and she could
not bear it easily.   But when she discovered, half an
hour later, that the guards were obeying the Great
King's orders, she bowed her head silently and went to
her apartments to consider what she should do.

She could do nothing.   There was no appeal against
the king's word.   He had distinctly commanded that
no one save Nehushta, not even Atossa herself, was to
be allowed to enter ; he had placed the guards there
himself the previous day, and had himself given the
order.

K

For eleven days the door was barred; but Atossa
did not again attempt to enter.   Darius would have
visited roughly such an offence, and she knew how
delicate her position was.   She resigned herself and
occupied her mind with other things.   Daily, an hour
before noon, Nehushta swept proudly through the gate,
and disappeared among the roses and myrtles of the
garden; and daily, precisely as the sun reached the
meridian, the king went in between the spearmen, and
disappeared in like manner.

Darius had grown so suddenly stern and cold in
manner towards the queen, that she dared not even
mention the subject of the garden to him, fearing a
sudden outburst of his anger, which would surely put
an end to her existence in the court, and very likely to
her life.

As for Nehushta, she had plentiful cause for reflection and much time for dreaming.   If the days were
not happy, they were at least made bearable for her by
the absolute liberty she enjoyed.   The king would
have given her slaves and jewels and rich gifts without end, had she been willing to accept them.   She
said she had all she needed—and she said it a little
proudly; only the king's visits grew to be the centre
of the day, and each day the visit lengthened, till it
came to be nearly evening when Darius issued from
the gate.

She always waited for him in the eight-sided
pavilion, and as their familiarity grew, the king would
not even permit her to rise when he came, nor to use
any of those forms of the court speech which were so
distasteful to him.   He simply sat himself down beside her, and talked to her and listened to her answers,
as though he were one of his own subjects, no more

hampered by the cares and state of royalty than any soldier in the kingdom.

It was a week since Zoroaster had mounted to ride to Ecbatana, and Darius sat as usual upon the marble bench by the side of Nehushta, who rested among the cushions, talking now without constraint upon all matters that chanced to occur as subjects of conversation. She thought Darius was more silent than usual, and his dark face was pale. He seemed weary, as though from some great struggle, and presently Nehushta stopped speaking and waited to see whether the king would say anything.

During the silence nothing was heard saving the plash of the little fountain, and the low soft ripple of the tiny waves that rocked themselves against the edge of the basin.

"Do you know, Nehushta," he said at last, in a weary voice, "that I am doing one of the worst actions of my life?"

Nehushta started, and the shadows in her face grew darker.

"Say rather the kindest action you ever did," she murmured.

"If it is not bad, it is foolish," said Darius, resting his chin upon his hand and leaning forward. "I would rather it were foolish than bad—I fear me it is both."

Nehushta could guess well enough what it was he would say. She knew she could have turned the subject, or laughed, or interrupted him in many ways; but she did none of these things. An indescribable longing seized her to hear him say that he loved her. What could it matter? He was so loyal and good that he could never be more than a friend. He was the king of the world—had he not been honest and kind, he would have needed no wooing to do as he pleased to do, utterly and entirely. A word from his lips and the name of Zoroaster would be but the memory of a man dead; and again a word, and Nehushta would be the king's wife! What need had he of concealment, or of devious ways? He was the king of the earth, whose shadow was life and death, whose slightest wish was a law to be enforced by hundreds of thousands of warriors! There was nothing between him and his desires—nothing but that inborn justice and truth, in which he so royally believed. Nehushta felt that she could trust him, and she longed —out of mere curiosity, she thought—to hear him speak words of love to her. It would only be for a moment—they would be so soon spoken; and at her desire, he would surely not speak them again. It seemed so sweet, she knew not why, to make this giant of despotic power do as she pleased; to feel that she could check him, or let him speak—him whom all obeyed and feared, as they feared death itself.

She looked up quietly, as she answered :

"How can it be either bad or foolish of you to make others so happy?"

"It seems as though it could be neither—and yet, all my reason tells me it is both," replied the king earnestly. "Here I sit beside you, day after day, deceiving myself with the thought that I am making your time pass pleasantly till——"

"There is not any deception in that," interrupted Nehushta gently. Somehow she did not wish him to pronounce Zoroaster's name. "I can never tell you how grateful I am——"

"It is I who am grateful," interrupted the king in

his turn. "It is I who am grateful that I am allowed to be daily with you, and that you speak with me, and seem glad when I come——" He hesitated and stopped.

"What is there that is bad and foolish in that?" asked Nehushta, with a sudden smile, as she looked up into his face.

"There is more than I like to think," answered the king. "You say the time passes pleasantly for you. Do you think it is less pleasant for me?" His voice sank to a deep, soft tone, as he continued: "I sit here day after day, and day after day I love you more and more. I love you—where is the use of concealing that—if I could conceal it? You know it. Perhaps you pity me, for you do not love me. You pity me who hold the whole earth under my feet, forsooth, as an Egyptian juggler stands upon a ball, and rolls it whither he will." He ceased suddenly.

"Indeed I would that you did not love me," said Nehushta very gravely. She looked down. The pleasure of hearing the king's words was indeed exquisite, and she feared that her eyes might betray her. But she did not love him. She wondered what he would say next.

"You might as well wish that dry pastures should not burn when the sun shines on them, and there is no rain," he answered with a passing bitterness. "It is at least a satisfaction that my love does not harm you—that you are willing to have me for your friend——"

"Willing! Your friendship is almost the sweetest thing I know," exclaimed the princess. The king's eyes flashed darkly.

"Almost! Yes, truly—my friendship and another

man's love are the sweetest things! What would my
friendship be without his love? By Auramazda and
the six Amshaspands of Heaven, I would it weie m,
love and his friendship! I would that Zoroaster were
the king, and I Zoroaster, the king's servant! I would
give all Persia and Media, Babylon and Egypt, and all
the uttermost parts of my kingdom, to hear your sweet
voice say: 'Darius, I love thee!' I would give my
right hand, I would give my heart from my breast
and my soul from my body—my life and my strength,
and my glory and my kingdom would I give to hear
you say: 'Come, my beloved, and put thine arms
about me!' Ah, child! you know not what my love
is—how it is higher than the heavens in worshipping
you, and broader than the earth to be filled with you,
and deeper than the depths of the sea, to change not,
but to abide for you always."

The king's voice was strong, and the power of his
words found wings in it, and seemed to fly forth
irresistibly with a message that demanded an answer.
Nehushta regretted within herself that she had let him
speak—but for all the world she could not have given
up the possession of the words he had spoken. She
covered her eyes with one hand and remained silent—
for she could say nothing. A new emotion had got
possession of her, and seemed to close her lips.

"You are silent," continued the king. "You are
right. What should you answer me? My voice
sounds like the raving of a madman, chained by a chain
that he cannot break. If I had the strength of the
mountains, I could not move you. I know it. All
things I have but this—this love of yours that you
have given to another. I would I had it! I should
have the strength to surpass the deeds of men, had I

your love! Who is this whom you love? A captain?
A warrior? I tell you because you have so honoured
him, so raised him upon the throne of your heart, I
will honour him too, and I will raise him above all
men, and all the nation shall bow before him. I will
make a decree that he shall be worshipped as a god—
this man whom you have made a god of by your love.
I will build a great temple for you two, and I will go
up with all the people, and fall down and bow before
you, and worship you, and love you with every sinew
and bone of my body, and with every hope and joy
and sorrow of my soul. He whom you love shall ask,
and whatsoever he asks I will give to him and to you.
There shall not be anything left in the whole world
that you desire, but I will give it to you. Am I not
the king of the whole earth—the king of all living
things but you?"

Darius breathed savagely hard through his clenched
teeth, and rising suddenly, paced the pavement between
Nehushta and the fountain. She was silent still, overcome with a sort of terror at his words—words, every
one of which he was able to fulfil, if he so chose.
Presently he stood still before her.

"Said I not well, that I rave as a madman—that I
speak as a fool without understanding? What can I
give you that you want? Or what thing can I devise
that you have need of? Have you not all that the
world holds for mortal woman and living man? Do
you not love, and are you not loved in return? Have
you not all—all—all? Ah! woe is me that I am
lord over the nations, and have not a drop of the
waters of peace wherewith to quench the thirst of my
tormented soul! Woe is me that I rule the world and
trample the whole earth beneath my feet, and cannot

have the one thing that all the earth holds which is good! Woe is me, Nehushta, that you have cruelly stolen my peace from me, and I find it not—nor shall find it for evermore!"

The strong dark man stood wringing his hands together; his face was pale as the dead, his black eyes were blazing with a mad fire. Nehushta dared not look on the tempest she had roused, but she trembled and clasped her hands to her breast and looked down.

"Nay, you are right," he cried bitterly. "Answer me nothing, for you can have nothing to answer! Is it your fault that I am mad? Or is it your doing that I love you so? Has any one sinned in this? I have seen you—I saw you for a brief moment standing in the door of your tent—and seeing, I loved you, and love you, and shall love you till the heavens are rolled together and the scroll of all death is full! There is nothing, nothing that you can say or do. It is not your fault—it is not your sin; but it is by you and through you that I am undone,—broken as the tree in the storm of the mountains, burned up and parched as the beast perishing in the sun of the desert for lack of water, torn asunder and rent into pieces as the rope that breaks at the well! By you, and for you, and through you, I am ruined and lost—lost—lost for ever in the hell of my wretched greatness, in the immeasurable death of my own horrible despair!"

With a wild movement of agony, Darius fell at Nehushta's feet, prostrate upon the marble floor, and buried his face in the skirts of her mantle, utterly over-mastered and broken down by the tumult of his passion.

Nehushta was not heartless. Of a certainty she would have pitied any one in such distress and grief,

even had the cause thereof come less near to herself.
But, in all the sudden emotion she felt, the pity, the
fear, and the self-reproach, there was joined a vague
feeling that no man ever spoke as this man, that no
lover ever poured forth such abundant love before,
and in the dim suspicion of something greater than
she had ever known, her fear and her pity grew
stronger, and strove with each other.

At first she could not speak, but she put forth her
delicate hand and laid it tenderly on the king's
thick black hair, as gently as a mother might soothe
a passionate child; and he suffered it to rest there.
And presently she raised his head and laid it in her
lap, and smoothed his forehead with her soft fingers,
and spoke to him.

"You make me very sad," she almost whispered.
"I would that you might be loved as you deserve love
—that one more worthy than I might give you all I
cannot give."

He opened his dark eyes that were now dull and
weary, and he looked up to her face.

"There is none more worthy than you," he answered in low and broken tones.

"Hush," she said gently, "there are many. Will
you forgive me—and forget me? Will you blot out
this hour from your remembrance, and go forth and
do those great and noble deeds which you came into
the world to perform? There is none greater than
you, none nobler, none more generous."

Darius lifted his head from her knee, and sprang to
his feet.

"I will do all things, but I will not forget," he
said. "I will do the great and the good deeds,—for
you. I will be generous, for you; noble, for you;

while the world lasts my deeds shall endure; and
with them, the memory that they were done for you!
Grant me only one little thing."

"Ask anything—everything," answered Nehushta,
in troubled tones.

"Nehushta, you know how truly I love you—nay,
I will not be mad again; fear not! Tell me this—
tell me that if you had not loved Zoroaster, you would
have loved me."

Nehushta blushed deeply and then turned pale.
She rose to her feet, and took the king's outstretched
hands.

"Indeed, indeed, you are most worthy of love—
Darius, I could have loved you well." Her voice was
very low, and the tears stood in her eyes.

"The grace of the All-Wise God bless thee!" cried
the king, and it was as though a sudden bright light
shone upon his face. Then he kissed her two hands
fervently, and with one long look into her sorrowful
eyes, he turned and left her.

But no man saw the king that day, nor did any
know where he was, saving the two spearmen who
stood at the door of his chamber. Within, he lay upon
his couch, dry-eyed and stark, staring at the painted
carvings of the ceiling.

CHAPTER XI.

THE time passed, and it was eleven days since Zoroaster had set out. The king and Nehushta had continued to meet in the garden as before, and neither had ever referred to the day when the torrent of his heart had been suddenly let loose. The hours sped quietly and swiftly, without any event of importance. Only the strange bond, half friendship and half love, had grown stronger than before; and Nehushta wondered how it was that she could love two men so well, and yet so differently. Indeed they were very different men. She loved Zoroaster, and yet it sometimes seemed as though he would more properly have filled the place of a friend than of a lover. Darius she had accepted as her friend, but there were moments when she almost forgot that he was not something more. She tried to think of her meeting with Zoroaster, whether it would be like former meetings,—whether her heart would beat more strongly, or not beat at all when her lips touched his as of old. Her judgment was utterly disturbed and her heart no longer knew itself. She gave herself over to the pleasure of the king's society in the abandonment of the moment, half foreseeing that some great change was at hand, over which she could exercise no control.

The sun was just risen, but the bridge over the

quickly flowing Choaspes was still in the shadow cast over the plain by the fortress and the palace, when two horsemen appeared upon the road from Nineveh, riding at full gallop, and, emerging from the blue mist that still lay over the meadows, crossed the bridge and continued at full speed towards the ascent to the palace.

The one rider was a dark, ill-favoured man, whose pale flaccid cheeks and drooping form betrayed the utmost fatigue. A bolster was bound across the withers of his horse and another on the croup, so that he sat as in a sort of chair, but he seemed hardly able to support himself even with this artificial assistance, and his body swayed from side to side as his horse bounded over the sharp curve at the foot of the hill. His mantle was white with dust, and the tiara upon his head was reduced to a shapeless and dusty piece of crumpled linen, while his uncurled hair and tangled beard hung forward together in disorderly and dust-clotted ringlets.

His companion was Zoroaster, fair and erect upon his horse, as though he had not ridden three hundred farsangs in eleven days. There was dust indeed upon his mantle and garments, as upon those of the man he conducted, but his long fair hair and beard blew back from his face as he held his head erect to the breeze he made in riding, and the light steel cap was bright and burnished on his forehead. A slight flush reddened his pale cheeks as he looked upward to the palace, and thought that his ride was over and his errand accomplished. He was weary, almost to death; but his frame was elastic and erect still.

As they rode up the steep, the guards at the outer gate, who had already watched them for twenty minutes as they came up the road, mere moving specks under the white mist, shouted to those within that Zoroaster was returning, and the officer of the gate went at once to announce his coming to the king. Darius himself received the message, and followed the officer down the steps to the tower of the gateway, reaching the open space within, just as the two riders galloped under the square entrance and drew rein upon the pavement of the little court. The spearmen sprang to their feet and filed into rank as the cry came down the steps that the king was approaching, and Zoroaster leaped lightly from his horse, and bid Phraortes do likewise; but the wretched Median could scarce move hand or foot without help, and would have fallen head-long, had not two stout spearmen lifted him to the ground, and held him upon his legs.

Darius marched quickly up to the pair and stood still, while Zoroaster made his brief salutation. Phraortes, who between deadly fatigue and deadly fear of his life, had no strength left in him, fell forward upon his knees as the two soldiers relaxed their hold upon his arms.

"Hail, king of kings! Live for ever!" said Zoroaster. "I have fulfilled thy bidding. He is alive."

Darius laughed grimly as he eyed the prostrate figure of the Median.

"Thou art a faithful servant, Zoroaster," he answered, "and thou ridest as the furies that pursue the souls of the wicked—as the devils of the mountains after a liar. He would not have lasted much farther, this bundle of sweating dust. Get up, fellow!" he said, touching Phraortes's head with his toe. "Thou liest grovelling there like a swine in a ditch."

The soldiers raised the exhausted man to his feet. The king turned to Zoroaster.

"Tell me, thou rider of whirlwinds," he said, laughing, "will a man more readily tell the truth, or speak lies, when he is tired?"

"A man who is tired will do whichever will procure him rest," returned Zoroaster, with a smile.

"Then I will tell this fellow that the sooner he speaks the truth the sooner he may sleep," said the king. Going near to Zoroaster, he added in an undertone: "Before thou thyself restest, go and tell the queen privately that she send away her slaves, and await me and him thou hast brought in a few minutes. This fellow must have a little refreshment, or he will die upon the steps."

Zoroaster turned and went up the broad stairs, and threaded the courts and passages, and mounted to the terrace where he had first met Atossa before the king's apartments. There was no one there, and he was about to enter under the great curtain, when the queen herself came out and met him face to face. Though it was yet very early, she was attired with more than usual care, and the faint colours of her dress and the few ornaments she wore, shone and gleamed brightly in the level beams of the morning sun. She had guessed that Zoroaster would return that day, and she was prepared for him.

As she came suddenly upon him, she gave a little cry, that might well have been feigned.

"What! Are you already returned?" she asked, and the joy her voice expressed was genuine. He looked so godlike as he stood there in the sunlight— her heart leaped for the joy of only seeing him.

"Yes—I bear this message from the Great King to

the queen. The Great King commands that the queen send away her slaves, and await the king and him I have brought with me, in the space of a few minutes."

"It is well," answered Atossa. "There are no slaves here and I await the king." She was silent a moment. "Are you not glad to have come back?" she asked, presently.

"Yes," said Zoroaster, whose face brightened quickly as he spoke. "I am indeed glad to be here again. Would not any one be glad to have finished such a journey?"

The queen stood with her back to the curtained doorway and could see down the whole length of the balcony to the head of the staircase. Zoroaster faced her and the door. As he spoke, Atossa's quick eyes caught sight of a figure coming quickly up the last steps of the stairway. She recognised Nehushta instantly, but no trembling of her lids or colouring of her cheek, betrayed that she had seen the approach of her enemy. She fixed her deep-blue eyes upon Zoroaster's, and gazing somewhat sadly, she spoke in low and gentle tones:

"The time has seemed long to me since you rode away, Zoroaster," she said.

Zoroaster, astonished at the manner in which she spoke, turned pale, and looked down coldly at her beautiful face. At that moment Nehushta stepped upon the smooth marble pavement of the balcony.

Still Atossa kept her eyes fixed on Zoroaster's.

"You answer me nothing?" she said in broken tones. Then suddenly, as though acting under an irresistible impulse, she threw her arms wildly about his neck and kissed him passionately again and again.

"Oh Zoroaster, Zoroaster, my beloved!" she cried.

"you must never, never leave me again!" And again she kissed him, and fell forward upon his breast, holding him so tightly that, for a moment, he did not know which way to move. He put his hands upon her shoulders, to her waist—to try to push her from him. But it was in vain; she clung to him desperately and sobbed upon his breast.

In the sudden and fearful embarrassment in which he was placed, he did not hear a short, low groan far off behind him, nor the sound of quickly retreating steps upon the stairs. But Atossa heard and rejoiced fiercely; and when she looked up, Nehushta was gone, with the incurable wound in her breast.

Atossa suddenly let her arms fall from the warrior's neck, looked into his eyes once, and then, with a short, sharp cry, she buried her face in her hands and leaned back against the door-post by the heavy striped curtain.

"Oh, my God! What have I done?" she moaned.

Zoroaster stood for one moment in hesitation and doubt. It seemed as though he had received a sudden revelation of numberless things he had never understood. He spoke quietly, at last, with a great effort, and his voice sounded kindly.

"I thank the good powers that I do not love thee—and I would that thou didst not love me. For I am the Great King's servant, faithful to death—and if I loved thee I should be a liar, and a coward, and the basest of all mankind. Forget, I pray thee, that thou hast spoken, and let me depart in peace. For the Great King is at hand, and thou must not suffer that he find thee weeping, lest he think thou fearest to meet Phraortes the Median face to face. Forget, I pray thee—and forgive thy servant if he have done anything amiss."

Atossa looked up suddenly. Her eyes were bright and clear, and there was not a trace of tears in them. She laughed harshly.

"I—weep before the king! You do not know me. Go, if thou wilt. Farewell, Zoroaster,"—her voice softened a little,—"farewell. It may be that you shall live, but it may be that you shall die, because I love you."

Zoroaster bent his head in respectful homage, and turned and went his way. The queen looked after him, and as he disappeared upon the staircase, she began to smooth her head-dress and the locks of her golden hair, and for a moment, she smiled sweetly to herself.

"That was a mortal wound, well dealt," she said aloud. But as she gazed out over the city, her face grew grave and thoughtful. "But I do love him," she added softly, "I do—I do—I loved him long ago." She turned quickly, as though fearing some one had overheard her. "How foolish I am!" she exclaimed impatiently; and she turned and passed away under the heavy curtain, leaving the long balcony once more empty,—save for the rush of a swallow that now and then flew in between the pillars, and hovered for a moment high up by the cornice, and sped out again into the golden sunshine of the summer morning.

Zoroaster left Atossa with the hope of finding some means of seeing Nehushta. But it was impossible. He knew well that he could not so far presume as to go to her apartment by the lower passage where he had last seen her on the day of his departure for Ecbatana, and the slave whom he despatched from the main entrance of the women's part of the palace returned with the brief information that Nehushta

was alone in her chamber, and that no one dared
disturb her.

Worn out with fatigue and excitement, and scarcely
able to think connectedly upon the strange event of
the morning, Zoroaster wearily resigned himself to
seeing Nehushta at a later hour, and entering his own
cool chamber, lay down to rest. It was evening when
he awoke.

Meanwhile the king commanded that Phraortes
should be fed and refreshed, and immediately brought
to the queen's apartment. Half an hour after Zoroaster
had left her, Atossa was in the chamber which was
devoted to her toilet. She sat alone before her great
silver mirror, calmly awaiting the turn of events.
Some instinct had told her that she would feel stronger
to resist an attack in the sanctuary of her small inner
room, where every object was impregnated with her
atmosphere, and where the lattices of the two windows
were so disposed that she would be able to see the
expression of her adversaries without exposing her own
face to the light.

She leaned forward and looked closely at herself in
the glass, and with a delicate brush of camel's hair
smoothed one eyebrow that was a little ruffled. It
had touched Zoroaster's tunic when she threw herself
upon his breast ; she looked at herself with a genuine
artistic pleasure, and smiled.

Before long she heard the sound of leathern shoes
upon the pavement outside, and the curtain was
suddenly lifted. Darius pushed Phraortes into the
room by the shoulders and made him stand before the
queen. She rose and made a salutation, and then sat
down again in her carved chair. The king threw
himself upon a heap of thick, hard cushions that

formed a divan on one side of the room, and prepared to watch attentively the two persons before him.

Phraortes, trembling with fear and excessive fatigue, fell upon his knees before Atossa, and touched the floor with his forehead.

"Get upon thy feet, man," said the king shortly, " and render an account of the queen's affairs."

" Stay," said Atossa, calmly, " for what purpose has the Great King brought this man before me ?"

"For my pleasure," answered Darius. " Speak fellow! Render thy account, and if I like not the manner of thy counting, I will crucify thee."

"The king liveth for ever," said Phraortes feebly, his flaccid cheeks trembling, as his limbs moved uneasily.

"The queen also liveth for ever," remarked Darius. " What is the state of the queen's lands at Ecbatana ?"

At this question Phraortes seemed to take courage, and began a rapid enumeration of the goods, cattle and slaves.

"This year I have sown two thousand acres of wheat which will soon be ripe for the harvest. I have sown also a thousand acres with other .grain. The fields of water-melons are yielding with amazing abundance since I caused the great ditches to be dug last winter towards the road. As for the fruit trees and the vine lands, they are prospering; but at present we have not had rain to push the first budding of the grapes. The olives will doubtless be very abundant this year, for last year there were few, as is the manner with that fruit. As for the yielding of these harvests of grain and wine and oil and fruit, I doubt not that the whole sales will amount to an hundred talents of gold."

" Last year they only yielded eighty-five," remarked
the queen, who had affected to listen to the whole
account with the greatest interest.   " I am well pleased,
Phraortes.   Tell me of the cattle and sheep—and of
the slaves; whether many have died this year."

" There are five hundred head of cattle, and one
hundred calves dropped in the last two months.
From the scarcity of rain this year, the fodder has
been almost destroyed, and there is little hay from the
winter.   I have, therefore, sent great numbers of slaves
with camels to the farther plains to eastward, whence
they return daily with great loads of hay—of a coarse
kind, but serviceable.   As for the flocks, they are now
pasturing for the summer upon the slopes of the Zagros
mountains.   There were six thousand head of sheep
and two thousand head of goats at the shearing in the
spring, and the wool is already sold for eight talents.
As for the slaves, I have provided for them after a
new fashion.   There were many young men from the
captives that came after the war two years ago.   For
these I have purchased wives of the dealers from
Scythia.   These Scythians sell all their women at a
low price.   They are hideous barbarians, speaking a
strange tongue, but they are very strong and enduring,
and I doubt not they will multiply exceedingly and
bring large profits——"

" Thou art extraordinarily fluent in thy speech,"
interrupted the king.   " But there are details that the
queen wishes to know.   Thou art aware that in a
frontier country like the province of Ecbatana, it is
often necessary to protect the crops and the flocks
from robbers.   Hast thou therefore thought of arming
any of these slaves for this purpose ?"

" Let not the king be angry with his servant,"

returned Phraortes, without hesitation "There are many thousand soldiers of the king in Ecbatana, and the horsemen traverse the country continually. I have not armed any of the slaves, for I supposed we were safe in the protection of the king's men. Nevertheless, if the Great King command me——"

"Thou couldst arm them immediately, I suppose?" interrupted Darius. He watched Atossa narrowly ; her face was in the shadow.

"Nay," replied Phraortes, "for we have no arms. But if the king will give us swords and spear-heads——"

"To what end ?" asked Atossa. She was perfectly calm since she saw that there was no fear of Phraortes making a mistake upon this vital point. "What need have I of a force to protect lands that are all within a day's journey of the king's fortress ? The idea of carrying weapons would make all the slaves idle and quarrelsome. Leave them their spades and their ploughs, and let them labour while the soldiers fight. How many slaves have I now, Phraortes ?"

"There were, at the last return, fourteen thousand seven hundred and fifty-three men, ten thousand two hundred and sixteen women, and not less than five thousand children. But I expect——"

"What can you do with so many ?" asked Darius, turning sharply to the queen.

"Many of them work in the carpet-looms," answered Phraortes. "The queen receives fifty talents yearly from the sales of the carpets."

"All the carpets in the king's apartments are made in my looms," said Atossa, with a smile. "I am a great merchant."

"I have no doubt I paid you dearly enough for

them, too," said the king, who was beginning to be weary of the examination. He had firmly expected that either the Median agent, or the queen herself, would betray some emotion at the mention of arming the slaves, for he imagined that if Atossa had really planned any outbreak, she would undoubtedly have employed the large force of·men she had at her disposal, by finding them weapons and promising them their liberty in the event of success.

He was disappointed at the appearance of the man Phraortes. He had supposed him a strong, determined man of imperious ways and turbulent instincts, who could be easily led into revolution and sedition from the side of his ambition. He saw before him the traditional cunning, quick-witted merchant of Media, pale-faced and easily frightened; no more capable of a daring stroke of usurpation than a Jewish pedlar of Babylon. He was evidently a mere tool in the hands of the queen; and Darius stamped impatiently upon the floor when he thought that he had perhaps been deceived after all—that the queen had really written to Phraortes simply on account of her property, and that there was no revolution at all to be feared. Impulsive to the last degree. when the king had read the letter to Phraortes, his first thought had been to see the man for himself, to ask him a few questions and to put him at once to death if he found him untruthful. The man had arrived, broken with excessive fatigue and weak from the fearful journey; but under the very eye of the king, he had nevertheless given a clear and concise account of himself; and, though he betrayed considerable fear, he gave no reason for supposing that what he said was not true. As for the queen, she sat calmly by, polishing her nails with a small instrument of ivory, occasionally asking a question, or making a remark, as though it were all the most natural occurrence in the world.

Darius was impetuous and fierce. His intuitive decisions were generally right, and he acted upon them instantly, without hesitation; but he had no cunning and little strategy. He was always for doing and never for waiting; and to the extreme rapidity of his movements he owed the success he had. In the first three years of his reign he fought nineteen battles and vanquished nine self-styled kings; but he never, on any occasion, detected a conspiracy, nor destroyed a revolution before it had broken out openly. He was often, therefore, at the mercy of Atossa and frequently found himself baffled by her power of concealing a subtle lie under the letter of truth, and by her supreme indifference and coldness of manner under the most trying circumstances. In his simple judgment it was absolutely impossible for any one to lie directly without betraying some hesitation, and each time he endeavoured to place Atossa in some difficult position, when she must, he thought, inevitably betray herself, he was met by her inexplicable calm; which he was forced to attribute to the fact that she was in the right —no matter how the evidence might be against her.

The king decided that he had made a mistake in the present instance and that Phraortes was innocent of any idea of revolution. He could not conceive how such a man should be capable of executing a daring stroke of policy. He determined to let him go.

" You ought to be well satisfied with the result of these accounts," he said, staring hard at Atossa. " You

see you know more of your affairs, and sooner, than
you could have known if you had sent your letter.
Let this fellow go, and tell him to send his accounts
regularly in future, or he will have the pains of riding
hither in haste to deliver them. Thou mayest go now
and take thy rest," he added, rising and pushing the
willing Phraortes before him out of the room.

"Thou hast done well. I am satisfied with thee,
Phraortes," said Atossa coldly.

Once more the beautiful queen was left alone, and
once more she looked at herself in the silver mirror,
somewhat more critically than before. It seemed to
her as she gazed and turned first one side of her face
to the light and then the other, that she was a shade
paler than usual. The change would have been imperceptible to any one else, but she noticed it with a
little frown of disapproval. But presently she smoothed
her brow and smiled happily to herself. She had sus-
tained a terrible danger successfully.

She had hoped to have been able to warn Phraortes
how to act; but, partly because the meeting had taken
place so soon after his arrival, and partly because she
had employed a portion of that brief interval with
Zoroaster and in the scene she had suddenly invented
and acted, she had been obliged to meet her chief
agent without a moment's preparation, and she knew
enough of his cowardly character to fear lest he should
betray her and throw himself upon the king's mercy as
a reward for the information he could give. But the
crucial moment had passed successfully and there was
nothing more to fear. Atossa threw herself upon the
couch where the king had sat, and abandoned herself
to the delicious contemplation of the pain she must
have given in showing herself to Nehushta in Zoro-

aster's arms.   She was sure that as the princess could not have seen Zoroaster's face, she must have thought that it was he who was embracing the queen. She must have suffered horribly, if she really loved him !

CHAPTER XII.

WHEN Darius left the queen, he gave over the miserable Phraortes to the guards, to be cared for, and bent his steps towards the gardens. It was yet early, but he wished to be alone, and he supposed that Nehushta would come there before noon, as was her wont. Meanwhile, he wished to be free of the court and of the queen. Slowly he entered the marble gate and walked up the long walk of roses, plucking a leaf now and then, and twisting it in his fingers, scenting the fresh blossoms with an almost boyish gladness, and breathing in all the sweet warmth of the summer morning. He had made a mistake, and he was glad to be away, where he could calmly reflect upon the reason of his being deceived.

He wandered on until he came to the marble pavilion, and would have gone on to stray farther into the gardens, but that he caught sight of a woman's mantle upon the floor as he passed by the open doorway. He went up the few steps and entered.

Nehushta lay upon the marble pavement at her full length, her arms extended above her head. Her face was ghastly pale and her parted lips were white. She looked as one dead. Her white linen tiara had almost fallen from her heavy hair, and the long black locks streamed upon the stone in thick confusion. Her fingers were tightly clenched, and on her face was such an expression of agony, as Darius had never dreamed of, nor seen in those dead in battle.

The king started back in horror as he caught sight of the prostrate figure. He thought she was dead—murdered, perhaps—until, as he gazed, he saw a faint movement of breathing. Then he sprang forward, and kneeled, and raised her head upon his knee, and chafed her temples and her hands. He could reach the little fountain as he knelt, and he gathered some water in his palm and sprinkled it upon her face.

At last she opened her eyes—then closed them wearily again—then opened them once more in quick astonishment, and recognised the king. She would have made an effort to rise, but he checked her, and she let her head sink back upon his knee. Still he chafed her temples with his broad, brown hand, and gazed with anxious tenderness into her eyes, that looked at him for a moment, and then wandered and then looked again.

"What is this?" she asked, vacantly, at last.

"I know not," answered the king. "I found you here—lying upon the floor. Are you hurt?" he asked tenderly.

"Hurt? No—yes, I am hurt—hurt even to death," she added suddenly. "Oh, Darius, I would I could tell you! Are you really my friend?"

She raised herself without his help and sat up. The hot blood rushed back to her cheeks and her eyes regained their light.

"Can you doubt that I am your friend, your best friend?" asked the king.

Nehushta rose to her feet and paced the little hall in great emotion. Her hands played nervously with the golden tassels of her mantle, her head-dress had fallen quite back upon her shoulders, and the masses of her hair were let loose. From time to time she glanced at the king, who eyed her anxiously as he stood beside the fountain.

Presently she stopped before him, and very gravely fixed her eyes on him.

"I will tell you something," she said, beginning in low tones. "I will tell you this—I cannot tell you all. I have been horribly deceived, betrayed, made a sport of. I cannot tell you how—you will believe me, will you not? This man I loved—I love him not—has cast me off as an old garment, as a thing of no price—as a shoe that is worn out and that is not fit for his feet to tread upon. I love him not—I hate him —oh, I love him not at all!"

Darius's face grew dark and his teeth ground hard together, but he stood still, awaiting what she should say. But Nehushta ceased, and suddenly she began again to walk up and down, putting her hand to her temples, as though in pain. Once more she paused, and, in her great emotion laid her two hands upon the shoulder of the king, who trembled at her touch, as though a strong man had struck him.

"You said you loved me, once," said Nehushta, in short, nervous tones, almost under her breath. "Do you love me still?"

"Is it so long since I told you I loved you?" asked Darius, with a shade of bitterness. "Ah! do not tempt me—do not stir my sickness. Love you? Yea—as the earth loves the sun—as man never loved woman. Love you? Ay! I love you, and I am the most miserable of men." He shook from head to foot with strong emotion, and the stern lines of his face darkened as he went on speaking. "Yet, though I love you so, I cannot harm him,—for my great oath's sake I cannot—yet for you, almost I could. Ah Nehushta, Nehushta!" he cried passionately, "tempt me not! Ask me not this, for you can almost make a liar of the Great King if you will!"

"I tempt you not," answered the princess. "I will not that you harm a hair of his head. He is not worthy that you should lift the least of your fingers to slay him. But this I tell you——" she hesitated. The king in his violent excitement, as though foreseeing what she would say, seized her hands and held them tightly while he gazed into her eyes.

"Darius," she said, almost hurriedly, "if you love me, and if you desire it, I will be your wife."

A wild light broke from the king's eyes. He dropped her hands and stepped backwards from her, staring hard. Then, with a quick motion, he turned and threw himself upon the marble seat that ran around the hall, and buried his face and sobbed aloud.

Nehushta seemed to regain some of her calmness, when once she had said the fatal words. She went and knelt beside him and smoothed his brow and wild, rough hair. The great tears stained his dark cheek. He raised himself and looked at her and put one arm about her neck.

"Nehushta" he whispered, "is it true?"

She bowed her head silently. Darius drew her towards him and laid her cheek upon his breast. His face bent down to hers, most tenderly, as though he would have kissed her. But suddenly he drew back, and turned his eyes away.

"No," he said, as though he had regained the mastery over himself. "It is too much to ask—that

I might kiss you! It is too much—too much—that you give me. I am not worthy that you should be my wife. Nay!" he cried, as she would not let him rise from his seat. "Nay, let me go, it is not right—it is not worthy—I must not see you any more. Oh, you have tempted me till I am too weak——"

"Darius, you are the noblest of men, the best and bravest." Then with a sudden impulse it seemed to Nehushta that she really loved him. The majestic strength of Zoroaster seemed cold and meaningless beside the fervour of the brave young king, striving so hard to do right under the sorest temptation, striving to leave her free, even against her will. For the moment she loved him, as such women do, with a passionate impulse. She put her arms about him and drew him down to her.

"Darius, it is truth—I never loved you, but I love you now, for, of all living men, you have the bravest heart." She pressed a kiss hotly upon his forehead and her head sank upon his shoulder. For one moment the king trembled, and then, as though all resistance were gone from him, his arms went round her, locking with hers that held him, and he kissed her passionately.

When Zoroaster awoke from his long sleep it was night. He had dreamed evil dreams, and he woke with a sense of some great disaster impending. He heard unwonted sounds in the hall outside his chamber, and he sprang to his feet and called one of the soldiers of his guard.

"What is happening?" asked Zoroaster quickly.

"The Great King, who lives for ever, has taken a new wife to-day," answered the soldier, standing erect, but eyeing Zoroaster somewhat curiously. Zoroaster's heart sank within him.

"What ? Who is she?" he asked, coming nearer to the man.

"The new queen is Nehushta—the Hebrew princess," answered the spearman. "There is a great banquet, and a feast for the guard, and much food and wine for the slaves——"

"It is well," answered Zoroaster. "Go thou, and feast with the rest."

The man saluted, and left the room. Zoroaster remained standing alone, his teeth chattering together and his strong limbs shaking beneath him. But he abandoned himself to no frenzy of grief, nor weeping ; one seeing him would have said he was sick of a fever. His blue eyes stared hard at the lamp-light and his face was, white, but he did not so much as utter an exclamation, nor give one groan. He went and sat down upon a chair and folded his hands together, as though waiting for some event. But nothing happened; no one came to disturb him in his solitude, though he could hear the tramping feet and the unceasing talk of the slaves and soldiers without. In the vast palace, where thousands dwelt, where all were feasting or talking of the coming banquet, Zoroaster was utterly alone.

At last he rose, slowly, as though with an effort, and paced twice from one end of the room to the other. Upon a low shelf on one side, his garments were folded together, while his burnished cuirass and helmet and other arms which he had not worn upon his rapid journey to Ecbatana, hung upon nails in the wall above. He looked at all these things and turned the clothes over piece by piece, till he had found a great dark mantle and a black hood such as was worn in Media. These he put on, and beneath the cloak he girded a broad, sharp knife about him. Then wrapping himself closely round with the dark-coloured stuff and drawing the hood over his eyes, he lifted the curtain of his door and went out, without casting a look behind him.

In the crowd of slaves he passed unnoticed; for the hall was but dimly lighted by a few torches, and every one's attention was upon the doings of the day and the coming feast.

Zoroaster soon gathered from the words he heard spoken, that the banquet had not yet begun, and he hastened to the columned porch through which the royal party must pass on the way to the great hall which formed the centre of the main building. Files of spearmen, in their bronze breastplates and scarlet and blue mantles, lined the way, which was strewn with yellow sand and myrtle leaves and roses. At every pillar stood a huge bronze candlestick, in which a torch of wax and fir-gum burned, and flared, and sent up a cloud of half pungent, half aromatic smoke. Throngs of slaves and soldiers pressed close behind the lines of spearmen, elbowing each other with loud jests and surly complaints, to get a better place, a sea of moving, shouting, gesticulating humanity. Zoroaster's great height and broad shoulders enabled him easily to push to the front, and he stood there, disguised and unknown, peering between the heads of two of his own soldiers to obtain the first view of the procession as it came down the broad staircase at the end of the porch.

Suddenly the blast of deep-toned trumpets was heard in the distance, and silence fell upon the great multitude. With a rhythmic sway of warlike tone the clangour rose and fell, and rose again as the trumpeters came out upon the great staircase and began to descend. After them came other musicians, whose softer instruments began to be heard in harmony . with the resounding bass of the horns, and then, behind them, came singers, whose strong, high voices completed the full burst of music that went before the king.

With measured tread the procession advanced. There were neither priests, nor sacrificers, nor any connected with any kind of temple; but after the singers came two hundred noble children clad in white, bearing long garlands of flowers that trailed upon the ground, so that many of the blossoms were torn off and strewed the sand.

But Zoroaster looked neither on the singers, nor on the children. His eyes were fixed intently on the two figures that followed them—Darius, the king, and Nehushta, the bride. They walked side by side, and the procession left an open space, ten paces before and ten paces behind the royal pair. Darius wore the tunic of purple and white stripes, the mantle of Tyrian purple on his shoulders and upon his head the royal crown of gold surrounded the linen tiara; his left hand, bare and brown and soldier-like, rested upon the golden hilt of his sword, and in his right, as he walked, he carried a long golden rod surmounted by a ball, twined with myrtle from end to end. He walked proudly forward, and as he passed, many a spearman thought with pride that the Great King looked as much a soldier as he himself.

By his left side came Nehushta, clad entirely in cloth of gold, while a mantle of the royal purple hung down behind her. Her white linen tiara was bound round with myrtle and roses, and in her hands she bore a myrtle bough.

M

Her face was pale in the torchlight, but she seemed composed in manner, and from time to time she glanced at the king with a look which was certainly not one of aversion.

Zoroaster felt himself growing as cold as ice as they approached, and his teeth chattered in his head. His brain reeled with the smoke of the torches, the powerful, moving tones of the music and the strangeness of the whole sight. It seemed as though it could not be real. He fixed his eyes upon Nehushta, but his face was shaded all around by his dark hood. Nevertheless, so intently did he gaze upon her that, as she came near, she felt his look, as it were, and, searching in the crowd behind the soldiers, met his eyes. She must have known it was he, even under the disguise that hid his features, for, though she walked calmly on, the angry blood rushed to her face and brow, overspreading her features with a sudden, dark flush.

Just as she came up to where Zoroaster stood, he thrust his covered head far out between the soldiers. His eyes gleamed like coals of blue fire and his voice came low, with a cold, clear ring, like the blade of a good sword striking upon a piece of iron.

" Faithless ! "

That was all he said, but all around heard the cutting tone, that neither the voices of the singers, nor the clangour of the trumpets could drown.

Nehushta drew herself up and paused for one moment, and turned upon the dark-robed figure a look of such unutterable loathing and scorn as one would not have deemed could be concentrated in a human face. Then she passed on.

The two spearmen turned quickly upon the man between them, who had uttered the insult against the

new queen, and laid hold of him roughly by the
shoulders.   A moment more and his life would have
been ended by their swords.   But his strong, white
hands stole out like lightning, and seized each soldier
by the wrist, and twisted their arms so suddenly and
with such furious strength, that they cried aloud with
pain and fell headlong at his feet.   The people parted
for a space in awe and wonder, and Zoroaster turned,
with his dark mantle close drawn around him, and
strode out through the gaping crowd.

"It is a devil of the mountains!" cried one.

"It is Ahriman himself!" said another.

"It is the soul of the priest of Bel whom the king
slew at Babylon!"

"It is the Evil Spirit of Cambyses!"

"Nay," quoth one of the spearmen, rubbing his
injured hand, "it was Zoroaster, the captain.   I saw
his face beneath that hood he wore."

"It may be," answered his fellow.   "They say he
can break a bar of iron, as thick as a man's three
fingers, with his hand.   But I believe it was a devil
of the mountains."

But the procession marched on, and long before the
crowd had recovered enough from its astonishment to
give utterance to these surmises, Zoroaster had passed
out of the porch and back through the deserted courts,
and down the wide staircase to the palace gate, and
out into the quiet, starlit night, alone and on foot.

He would have no compromise with his grief; he
would be alone with it.   He needed not mortal
sympathy and he would not have the pity of man.
The blow had struck home with deadly certainty and
the wound was such as man cannot heal, neither
woman.   The fabric of happiness, which in a year he

had built himself, was shattered to its foundation, and the fall of it was fearful. The ruin of it reached over the whole dominion of his soul and rent all the palace of his body. The temple that had stood so fair, whither his heart had gone up to worship his beloved one, was destroyed and utterly beaten to pieces; and the ruin of it was as a heap of dead bones, so loathsome in decay, that the eyes of his spirit turned in horror and disgust from the inward contemplation of so miserable a sight.

Alone and on foot, he went upon his dreary way, dry-eyed and calm. There was nothing left of all his past life that he cared for. His armour hung in his chamber in the palace and with it he left the Zoroaster he had known—the strong, the young, the beautiful; the warrior, the lover, the singer of sweet songs, the smiter of swift blows, the peerless horseman, the matchless man. He who went out alone into the great night, was a moving sorrow, a horror of grief made visible as a walking shadow among things real, a man familiar already with death as with a friend, and with the angel of death as with a lover.

Alone—it was a beginning of satisfaction to be away from all the crowd of known and unknown faces familiar to his life—but the end and attainment of satisfaction could only come when he should be away from himself, from the heavy body that wearied him, and from the heavier soul that was crushed with itself as with a burden. For sorrow was his companion from that day forth, and grief undying was his counsellor.

Ah God! She was so beautiful and her love was so sweet and strong! Her face had been as the face of an angel, and her virgin-heart as the innermost leaves of the rose that are folded together in the bud before the rising of the sun. Her kiss was as the breath of spring that gladdens the earth into new life, her eyes as crystal wells, from the depths whereof truth rose blushing to the golden light of day. Her lips were so sweet that a man wondered how they could ever part, till, when they parted, her gentle breath bore forth the music of her words, that was sweeter than all created sounds. She was of all earthly women the most beautiful—the very most lovely thing that God had made; and of all mortal women that have loved, her love had been the purest, the gentlest, the truest. There was never woman like to her, nor would be again.

And yet—scarce ten days had changed her, had so altered and disturbed the pure elements of her wondrous nature that she had lied to herself and lied to her lover the very lie of lies—for what? To wear a piece of purple of a richer dye than other women wore, to bind her hair with a bit of gold, to be called a queen—a queen forsooth! when she had been from her birth up the sovereign queen of all created women!

The very lie of lies! Was there ever such a monstrous lie since the world first learned the untruths of the serpent's wisdom? Had she not sworn and promised, by the holiness of her God, to love Zoroaster for ever? For ever. O word, that had meant heaven, and now meant hell!—that had meant joy without any end and peace and all love!—that meant now only pain eternal, and sorrow, and gnawing torment of a wound that would never heal! O Death, that yesterday would have seemed Life for her! O Life, that to-day, by her, was made the Death of deaths!

Emptiness of emptiness—the whole world one hollow cavern of vanity—lifeless and lightless, where the

ghosts of the sorrows of men moan dismally, and the
shadows of men's griefs scream out their wild agony
upon the ghastly darkness! Night, through which no
dawn shall ever gleam, fleet and fair, to touch with
rosy fingers the eyes of a dead world and give them
sight! Winter, of unearthly cold, that through all the
revolving ages of untiring time, shall never see the face
of another spring, nor feel its icy veins thawing with
the pulses of a forgotten life, quickened from within
with the thrilling hope of a new and glorious birth!

Far out upon the southern plain Zoroaster lay upon
the dew-wet ground and gazed up into the measureless
depths of heaven, where the stars shone out like myriads
of jewels set in the dark mantle of night.

Gradually, as he lay, the tempest of his heart subsided, and the calm of the vast solitude descended upon
him, even as the dew had descended upon the earth.
His temples ceased to throb with the wild pulse that
sent lightnings through his brain at every beat, and
from the intensity of his sorrow, his soul seemed to
float upwards to those cool depths of the outer firmament where no sorrow is. His eyes grew glassy and
fixed, and his body rigid in the night-dews; and his
spirit, soaring beyond the power of earthly forces to
weigh down its flight, rose to that lofty sphere where
the morning and the evening are but one eternal day,
where the mighty unison of the heavenly chorus sends
up its grand plain-chant to God Most High.

CHAPTER XIII.

FAR in the wild mountains of the south, where a primeval race of shepherds pastures its flocks of shaggy goats upon the scanty vegetation of rocky slopes, there is a deep gorge whither men seldom penetrate, and where the rays of the sun fall but for a short hour at noonday. A man may walk, or rather climb, along the side of the little stream that rushes impetuously down among the black rocks, for a full hour and a half before he reaches the end of the narrow valley. Then he will come upon a sunken place, like a great natural amphitheatre, the steep walls of boulders rising on all sides to a lofty circle of dark crags. In the midst of this open space a spring rises suddenly from beneath a mass of black stone, with a rushing, gurgling sound, and makes a broad pool, whence the waters flow down in a little torrent through the gorge till they emerge far below into the fertile plain and empty themselves into the Araxes, which flows by the towers and palaces of lordly Stakhar, more than two days' journey from the hidden circle in the mountains.

It would have been a hard thing to recognise Zoroaster in the man who sat day after day beside the spring, absorbed in profound meditation. His tall figure was wasted almost to emaciation by fasting and exposure ; his hair and beard had turned snow-white,

and hung down in abundant masses to his waist, and
his fair young face was pale and transparent. But in
·his deep blue eyes there was a light different from
the light of other days—the strange calm fire of a
sight that looks on wondrous things, and sees what
the eyes of men may not see, and live.

Nearly three years had passed since he went forth
from the palace of Shushan, to wander southwards in
search of a resting-place, and he was but three-and-
thirty years of age. But between him and the past
there was a great gulf—the interval between the man
and the prophet, between the cares of mortality and
the divine calm of the higher life.

From time to time indeed, he ascended the steep
path he had made among the stones and rocks, to the
summit of the mountain; and there he met one of the
shepherds of the hills, who brought him once every
month a bag of parched grain and a few small, hard
cheeses of goats' milk; and in return for these scanty
provisions, he gave the man each time a link from the
golden chain he had worn and which was still about
his neck when he left the palace. Three-and-thirty
links were gone since he had come there, and the chain
was shorter by more than half its length. It would
last until the thousand days were accomplished, and
there would still be much left. Auramazda, the All-
Wise, would provide.

Zoroaster sat by the spring and watched the crystal
waters sparkle in the brief hour of sunshine at noonday, and turn dark and deep again when the light was
gone. He moved not through the long hours of day,
sitting as he had sat in that place now for three years
neither scorched by the short hours of sunlight, nor
chilled by winter's frost and snow. The wild long-

haired sheep of the mountain came down to drink at noon, and timidly gazed with their stupid eyes at the immovable figure; and at evening the long-bodied, fierce-eyed wolves would steal stealthily among the rocks and come and snuff the ground about his feet, presently raising their pointed heads with a long howl of fear, and galloping away through the dusk in terror, as though at something unearthly.

And when at last the night was come, Zoroaster arose and went to the spot where the rocks, over-hanging together, left a space through which one might enter; and the white-haired man gave one long look at the stars overhead, and disappeared within.

There was a vast cave, the roof reaching high up in a great vault; the sides black and polished, as though smoothed by the hands of cunning workmen; the floor a bed of soft, black sand, dry and even as the untrodden desert. In the midst, a boulder of black rock lay like a huge ball, and upon its summit burned a fire that was never quenched, and that needed no replenishing with fuel. The tall pointed flame shed a strangely white light around, that flashed and sparkled upon the smooth black walls of the cavern, as though they were mirrors. The flame also was immovable; it neither flickered, nor rose, nor fell; but stood as it were a spear-head of incandescent gold upon the centre of the dark altar. There was no smoke from that strange fire, nor any heat near it, as from other fires.

Then Zoroaster bent and put forth his forefinger and traced a figure upon the sand, which was like a circle, save that it was cut from north-west to south-east by two straight lines, and from north-east to south-west by two straight lines; and at each of the four small arcs, where the straight lines cut the circumference of the great circle, a part of a smaller circle outside the great one united the points over each other. And upon the east side, toward the altar, the great circle was not joined, but open for a short distance.[1]

When the figure was traced, Zoroaster came out from it and touched the black rock whereon the fire burned; and then he turned back and entered the circle, and with his fingers joined it where it was open on the east side through which he had entered. And immediately, as the circle was completed, there sprung up over the whole line he had traced a soft light; like that of the fire, but less strong. Then Zoroaster lay down upon his back, with his feet to the west and his head toward the altar, and he folded his hands upon his breast and closed his eyes. As he lay, his body became rigid and his face as the face of the dead; and his spirit was loosed in the trance and freed from the bonds of earth, while his limbs rested.

Lying there, separated from the world, cut off within the circle of a symbolised death by the light of the universal agent,[2] Zoroaster dreamed dreams and saw visions.

His mind was first opened to the understanding of those broader conceptions of space and time of which he had read in the books of Daniel, his master. He had understood the principles then, but he had not realised their truth. He was too intimately connected with the life around him, to be able to see in

[1] The Mazdayashnian Dakhma, or place of death. This figure represents the ground-plan of the modern Parsi Tower of Silence.

[2] The term "universal agent" has been used in the mysticism of ages, to designate that subtle and all-pervading fluid, of which the phenomena of light, heat, electricity and vitality are considered to be but the grosser and more palpable manifestations.

the clearer light which penetrates with universal truth all the base forms of perishable matter.

Daniel had taught him the first great principles. All men, in their ignorance, speak of the infinities of space and time as being those ideas which man cannot of himself grasp or understand. Man, they say, is limited in capacity; he can, therefore, not comprehend the infinite. A greater fault than this could not be committed by a thinking being. For infinity being unending, it is incapable of being limited; it rejects definition, which belongs, by its nature, to finite things. For definition means the placing of bounds, and that which is in-finite can have no bounds. The man, therefore, who seeks to bound what has no bounds, endeavours to define what is, by its nature, undefinable; and finding that the one poor means which he has of conveying fallacious impressions of illusory things to his mind through his deadened senses, is utterly insufficient to give him an idea of what alone is real, he takes refuge in his crass ignorance and coarse grossness of language, and asserts boldly that the human mind is too limited in its nature to conceive of infinite space, or of infinite time.

Not only is the untrammelled mind of man capable of these bolder conceptions, but even the wretched fool who sees in the material world the whole of what man can know, could never get so far as to think even of the delusive objects on which he pins his foolish faith, unless the very mind which he insults and misunderstands, had by its nature that infinite capacity of comprehension which, he says, exists not. For otherwise, if the mind be limited, there must be a definite limit to its comprehensive faculty, and it is easy to conceive that such a limit would soon become apparent to every student; as apparent as it is that a being, confined within three dimensions of space, cannot, without altering his nature, escape from these three dimensions, nor from the laws which govern matter having length, breadth and thickness alone, without the external fourth dimension, with its interchangeability of exterior and interior angles.

The very thought that infinite space cannot be understood, is itself a proof that the mind unconsciously realises the precise nature of such infinity, in attributing to it at once the all-comprehensiveness from which there is no escape, in which all dimensions exist, and by virtue of which all other conceptions become possible; since this infinite space contains in itself all dimensions of existence—transitory, real and potential; and if the capacity of the mind is co-extensive with the capacity of infinite space, since it feels itself undoubtedly capable of grasping any limited idea contained in any portion of the illimitable whole, it follows that the mind is of itself as infinite as the space in which all created things have their transitory form of being, and in which all uncreated truths exist eternally. The mind is aware of infinity by that true sort of knowledge which is an intimate conviction not dependent upon the operation of the senses.

Gradually, too, as Zoroaster fixed his intuition upon the first main principle of all possible knowledge, he became aware of the chief cause—of the universal principle of vivifying essence, which pervades all things, and in which arises motion as the original generator of transitory being. The great law of division became clear to him—the separation for a time of the universal agent into two parts, by the separation and reuniting of which comes light and heat and the hidden force

of life, and the prime rules of attractive action; all
things that are accounted material. He saw the
division of darkness and light, and how all things that
are in the darkness are reflected in the light; and how
the light which we call light is in reality darkness made
visible, whereas the true light is not visible to the eyes
that are darkened by the gross veil of transitory being.
And as from the night of earth, his eyes were gradually
opened to the astral day, he knew that the forms
that move and have being in the night are perishable and utterly unreal; whereas the purer being which
is reflected in the real light is true and endures for
ever.

Then, by his knowledge and power, and by the light
that was in him, he divided the portion of the universal
agent that was in the cave where he dwelt into two
portions, and caused them to reunite in the midst upon
the stone that was there; and the flame burned silently
and without heat upon his altar, day and night, without
intermission; and by the division of the power within
him, he could divide the power also that was latent in
other transitory beings, according to those laws which,
being eternal, are manifested in things not eternal, but
perishable.

And further, he meditated upon the seven parts of
man, and upon their separation, and upon the difference
of their nature.

For the first element of man is perishable matter.

And the second element of man is the portion of the
universal agent which gives him life.

And the third element of man is the reflection of
his perishable substance in the astral light, coincident
with him, but not visible to his earthly eye.

The fourth element of man is made up of all the

desires he feels by his material senses. This part is not real being, nor transitory being, but a result.

The fifth element of man is that which says: "I am," whereby a man knows himself from other men; and with it there is an intelligence of lower things, but no intelligence of things higher.

The sixth element is the pure understanding, eternal and co-extensive with all infinity of time and space—real, imperishable, invisible to the eye of man.

The seventh element is the soul from God.

Upon these things Zoroaster meditated long, and as his perishable body became weakened and emaciated with fasting and contemplation, he was aware that, at times, the universal agent ceased to be decomposed and recomposed in the nerves of his material part, so that his body became as though dead, and with it the fourth element which represents the sense of mortal desires; and he himself, the three highest elements of him,—his individuality, his intelligence and his soul,—became separated for a time from all that weighed them down; and his mind's eyes were opened, and he saw clearly in the astral light, with an intuitive knowledge of true things, and false.

And so, night after night, he lay upon the floor of his cavern, rigid and immovable; his body protected from all outer harmful influences by the circle of light he had acquired the power of producing. For though there was no heat in the flame, no mortal breathing animal could so much as touch it with the smallest part of his body without being instantly destroyed as by lightning. And so he was protected from all harm in his trances; and he left his body at will and returned to it, and it breathed again, and was alive.

So he saw into the past and into the present and into the future, and his soul was purified beyond the purity of man, and soared upwards, and dreamed of the eternal good and of the endless truth; and at last it seemed to him that he should leave his body in its trance, and never return to it, nor let it breathe again. For since it was possible thus to cast off mortality and put on immortality, it seemed to him that it was but a weariness to take up the flesh and wear it, when it was so easy to lay it down. Almost he had determined that he would then let death come, as it were unawares, upon his perishable substance, and remain for ever in the new life he had found.

But as his spirit thought in this wise, he heard a voice speaking to him, and he listened.

"One moment is as another, and there is no difference between one time and another time.

"One moment in eternity is of as great value as another moment, for eternity changes not, neither is one part of it better than another part.

"Though man be immortal as to his soul, he is mortal as to his body, and the time which his soul shall spend in his body is of as great worth to him as the time which he shall spend without it.

"Think not that by wilfully abandoning the body, even though you have the power and the knowledge to do so, you will escape from the state in which it has pleased God to put you.

"Rather shall your pain and the time of your suffering be increased, because you have not done with the body that which the body shall do.

"The life of the soul while it is in the body, has as much value as when it has left it. You shall not shorten the time of dwelling in the flesh.

"Though you know all things, you know not God. For though you know your body which is in the world, and the world which is in time, and time which is in space, yet your knowledge goeth no farther, for space and all that therein is, is in God.[1]

"You have learned earthly things and heavenly things. Learn then that you shall not escape the laws of earth while you are on earth, nor the laws of heaven when you are in heaven. Lift up your heart to God, but do in the body those things which are of the body.

"There are other men put into the world besides you. If you leave the world, what does your knowledge profit other men? And yet it is to profit other men that God has put you into the world.

"And not you only, but every man. The labour of man is to man, and the labour of angels to angels. But the time of man is as valuable in the sight of God, as the time of angels.

"All things that are not accomplished in their time shall be left unaccomplished for ever and ever. If while you are in the flesh, you accomplish not the things of the flesh after the manner of your humanity, you shall enter into the life of the spirit as one blind, or maimed; for your part is not fulfilled.

"Wisdom is this. A man shall not care for the things of the world for himself, and his soul shall be lifted and raised above all that is mean and perishable; but he shall perform his part without murmuring. He shall not forget the perishable things, though he soar to the imperishable.

"For man is to man as one portion of eternity to another; and as eternity would be imperfect if one moment could be removed, so also the earth would be

[1] Hermes Trismegistus, *Pœmandres* xi. 2.

imperfect if one man should be taken from it before his appointed time.

" If a man therefore take himself out of the world, he causes imperfection, and sins against perfection, which is the law of God.

" Though the world be in darkness, the darkness is necessary to the light. Though the world perish, and heaven perish not for ever, yet is the perishable necessary to the eternal.

" For the transitory and the unchangeable exist alike in eternity and are portions of it. And one moment is as another, and there is no difference between one time and another time.

" Go, therefore, and take up your body, and do with it the deeds of the body among men; for you have deeds to do, and unless they are done in their time, which is now, they will be unfulfilled for ever, and you will become an imperfect spirit.

" The imperfect spirit shall be finally destroyed, for nothing that is imperfect shall endure. To be perfect all things must be fulfilled, all deeds done, in the season while the spirit is in darkness with the body. The deeds perish, and the body which doeth them, but the soul of the perfect man is eternal, and the reflection of what he has done, abides for ever in the light.

" Hasten, for your time is short. You have learned all things that are lawful to be learnt, and your deeds shall be sooner accomplished.

" Hasten, for one moment is as another, and there is no difference between the value of one time and of another time.

" The moment which passes returns not, and the thing which a man should do in one time cannot be done in another time."

N

The voice ceased, and the spirit of Zoroaster returned
to his body in the cave, and his eyes opened. Then
he rose, and standing within the circle, cast sand upon
the portion towards the east; and so soon as the circle
was broken, it was extinguished and there remained
nothing but the marks Zoroaster had traced with his
fingers upon the black sand.

He drew his tattered mantle around him, and went
to the entrance of the cave, and passed out. And it
was night.

Overhead, the full moon cast her broad rays verti-
cally into the little valley, and the smooth black stones
gleamed darkly. The reflection caught the surface of
the little pool by the spring, and it was turned to a
silver shield of light.

Zoroaster came forward and stood beside the fountain, and the glory of the moon fell upon his white
locks and beard and on the long white hand he laid
upon the rock.

His acute senses, sharpened beyond those of men
by long' solitude and fasting, distinguished the step of
a man far up the height on the distant crags, and his
keen sight soon detected a figure descending cautiously,
but surely, towards the deep abyss where Zoroaster
stood. More and more clearly he saw him, till the
man was near, and stood upon an overhanging boulder
within speaking distance. He was the shepherd who,
from time to time, brought food to the solitary mystic;
and who alone, of all the goat-herds in those hills, would
have dared to invade the sacred precincts of Zoroaster's
retreat. He was a brave fellow, but the sight of the
lonely man by the fountain awed him; it seemed as
though his white hair emitted a light of its own
under the rays of the moon, and he paused in fear

lest the unearthly ascetic should do him some mortal hurt.

"Wilt thou harm me if I descend?" he called out timidly.

"I harm no man," answered Zoroaster. "Come in peace."

The active shepherd swung himself from the boulder, and in a few moments he stood among the stones at the bottom, a few paces from the man he sought. He was a dark fellow, clad in goat-skins, with pieces of leather bound around his short, stout legs. His voice was hoarse, perhaps with some still unconquered fear, and his staff rattled as he steadied himself among the stones.

"Art not thou he who is called Zoroaster?" he asked.

"I am he," answered the mystic. "What wouldest thou?"

"Thou knowest that the Great King with his queens and his court are at the palace of Stakhar," replied the man. "I go thither from time to time to sell cheeses to the slaves. The Great King has made a proclamation that whosoever shall bring before him Zoroaster shall receive a talent of gold and a robe of purple. I am a poor shepherd—fearest thou to go to the palace?"

"I fear nothing. I am past fear these three years."

"Will the Great King harm thee, thinkest thou? Thou hast paid me well for my pains since I first saw thee, and I would not have thee hurt."

"No man can harm me. My time is not yet come."

"Wilt thou go with me?" cried the shepherd, in sudden delight. "And shall I have the gold and the robe?"

"I will go with thee. Thou shalt have all thou

wouldest," answered Zoroaster.   "Art thou ready ?   I
have no goods to burden me."

"But thou art old," objected the shepherd, coming
nearer.   "Canst thou go so far on foot?   I have a
beast; I will return with him in the morning, and
meet thee upon the height.   I came hither in haste,
being but just returned from Stakhar with the news."

"I am younger than thou, though my hair is white.
I will go with thee.   Lead the way."

He stooped and drank of the fountain in the moonlight, from the hollow of his hand.   Then he turned,
and began to ascend the steep side of the valley.
The shepherd led the way in silence, overcome between
his awe of the man and his delight at his own good
fortune.

CHAPTER XIV.

It was now three years since Nehushta had been married to Darius, and the king loved her well. But often, in that time, he had been away from her, called to different parts of the kingdom by the sudden outbreaks of revolution which filled the early years of his reign. Each time he had come back in triumph, and each time he had given her some rich gift. He found indeed that he had no easy task to perform in keeping the peace between his two queens; for Atossa seemed to delight in annoying Nehushta and in making her feel that she was but the second in the king's favour, whatever distinctions might be offered her. But Darius was just and was careful that Atossa should receive her due, neither more nor less.

Nehushta was glad when Zoroaster was gone. She had suffered terribly in that moment when he had spoken to her out of the crowd, and the winged word had made a wound that rankled still. In those three years that passed, Atossa never undeceived her concerning the sight she had seen, and she still believed that Zoroaster had basely betrayed her. It was impossible, in her view, that it could be otherwise. Had she not seen him herself? Could any man do such an action who was not utterly base and heartless? She had, of course, never spoken to Darius of the scene upon the terrace. She did not desire the destruction of Atossa, nor of her faithless lover. Amid all the tender kindness the king lavished upon her, the memory of her first love endured still, and she could not have suffered the pain of going over the whole story again. He was gone, perhaps dead, and she would never see him again. He would not dare to set foot in the court. She remembered the king's furious anger against him, when he suspected that the hooded man in the procession was Zoroaster. But Darius had afterwards said, in his usual careless way, that he himself would have done as much, and that for his oath's sake, he would never harm the young Persian. By the grace of Auramazda he swore, he was the king of kings and did not make war upon disappointed lovers!

Meanwhile, Darius had built himself a magnificent palace, below the fortress of Stakhar, in the valley of the Araxes, and there he spent the winter and the spring, when the manifold cares of the state would permit him. He had been almost unceasingly at war with the numerous pretenders who set themselves up for petty kings in the provinces. With unheard-of rapidity, he moved from one quarter of his dominions to another, from east to west, from north to south; but each time that he returned, he found some little disturbance going on at the court, and he bent his brows and declared that a parcel of women were harder to govern than all Media, Persia, and Babylon together.

Atossa wearied him with her suggestions.

"When the king is gone upon an expedition," she said, "there is no head in the palace. Otanes is a weak man. The king will not give me the control of the household, neither will he give it to any one else."

"There is no one whom I can trust," answered Darius. "Can you not dwell together in peace for a month?"

"No," answered Atossa, with her winning smile, "it is impossible; the king's wives will never agree among themselves. Let the king choose some one and make a head over the palace."

"Whom shall I choose?" asked Darius, moodily.

"The king had a faithful servant once," suggested Atossa.

"Have I none now?"

"Yea, but none so faithful as this man of whom I speak, nor so ready to do the king's bidding. He departed from Shushan when the king took Nehushta to wife——"

"Mean you Zoroaster?" asked Darius, bending his brows, and eyeing Atossa somewhat fiercely. But she met his glance with indifference.

"The same," she answered. "Why not send for him and make him governor of the palace? He was indeed a faithful servant—and a willing one."

Still the king gazed hard at her face, as though trying to fathom the reason of her request, or at least to detect some scornful look upon her face to agree with her sneering words. But he was no match for the unparalleled astuteness of Atossa, though he had a vague suspicion that she wished to annoy him by calling up a memory which she knew could not be pleasant, and he retorted in his own fashion.

"If Zoroaster be yet alive I will have him brought, and I will make him governor of the palace. He was indeed a faithful servant—he shall rule you all and there shall be no more discord among you."

And forthwith the king issued a proclamation that

whosoever should bring Zoroaster before him should receive a talent of gold and a robe of purple as a reward.

But when Nehushta heard of it she was greatly troubled; for Atossa began to tell her that Zoroaster was to return and to be made governor of the palace; but Nehushta rose and left her forthwith, with such a look of dire hatred and scorn that even the cold queen thought she had, perhaps, gone too far.

There were other reasons why the king desired Zoroaster's return. He had often wondered secretly how the man could so have injured Nehushta as to turn her love into hate in a few moments; but he had never questioned her. It was a subject neither of them could have approached, and Darius was far too happy in his marriage to risk endangering that happiness by any untoward discovery. Nehushta's grief and anger had been so genuine when she told him of Zoroaster's treachery that it had never occurred to him that he might be injuring the latter in marrying the princess, though his generous heart had told him more than once, that Nehushta had married him half from gratitude for his kindness, and half out of anger with her false lover; but, capricious as she was in all other things, towards the king she was always the same, gentle and affectionate, though there was nothing passionate in her love. And now, the idea of seeing the man who had betrayed her installed in an official position in the palace, was terrible to her pride. She could not sleep for thinking how she should meet him, and what she should do. She grew pale and hollow-eyed with the anticipation of evil and all her peace went from her. Deep down in her heart there was yet a clinging affection for the old love, which she

smothered and choked down bravely; but it was there
nevertheless, a sleeping giant, ready to rise and overthrow her whole nature in a moment, if only she could
wash away the stain of faithlessness which sullied his
fair memory, and lift the load of dishonour which had
crushed him from the sovereign place he had held in
the dominion of her soul.

Darius was himself curious to ascertain the truth
about Zoroaster's conduct.   But another and a weightier
reason existed for which he wished him to return.
The king was disturbed about a matter of vital
importance to his kingdom, and he knew that, among
all his subjects, there was not one more able to give
him assistance and advice than Zoroaster, the pupil of
the dead prophet Daniel.

The religion of the kingdom was of a most uncertain
kind.   So many changes had passed over the various
provinces which made up the great empire that, for
generations, there had been almost a new religion for
every monarch.   Cyrus, inclining to the idolatry of
the Phœnicians, had worshipped the sun and moon,
and had built temples and done sacrifice to them and
to a multitude of deities.   Cambyses had converted the
temples of his father into places of fire-worship, and
had burnt thousands of human victims; rejoicing in
the splendour of his ceremonies and in the fierce love
of blood that grew upon him as his vices obtained the
mastery over his better sense.   But under both kings
the old Aryan worship of the Magians had existed
among the people, and the Magians themselves had
asserted, whenever they dared, their right to be considered the priestly caste, the children of the Brahmins
of the Aryan house.   Gomata—the false Smerdis
—was a Brahmin, at least in name, and probably

in descent; and during his brief reign the only decrees he issued from his retirement in the palace
of Shushan, were for the destruction of the existing
temples and the establishment of the Magian worship
throughout the kingdom. When Darius had slain
Smerdis, he naturally proceeded to the destruction
of the Magi, and the streets of Shushan ran with their
blood for many days. He then restored the temples
and the worship of Auramazda, as well as he was able;
but it soon became evident that the religion was in a
disorganised state and that it would be no easy matter
to enforce a pure monotheism upon a nation of men
who, in their hearts, were Magians, nature-worshippers;
and who, through successive reigns, had been driven
by force to the adoration of strange idols. It followed
that the people resisted the change and revolted whenever they could find a leader. The numerous revolutions, which cost Darius no less than nineteen battles,
were, almost without exception, brought about in the
attempt to restore the Magian worship in various
provinces of the kingdom, and it may well be doubted
whether, at any time in the world's history, an equal
amount of blood was ever shed in so short a period in
the defence of religious convictions.

Darius himself was a man who had the strongest
belief in the power of Auramazda, the All-Wise God,
and who did not hesitate to attribute all the evil in
the world to Ahriman, the devil. He had a bitter
contempt for all idolatry, nature-worship and super-
stition generally, and he adhered in his daily life to
the simple practices of the ancient Mazdayashnians.
But he was totally unfitted to be the head of a
religious movement; and, although he had collected
such of the priesthood as seemed most worthy, and had

built them temples and given them privileges of all
kinds, he was far from satisfied with their mode of
worship. He could not frame a new doctrine, but he
had serious doubts whether the ceremonies his priests
performed were as simple and religious as he wished
them to be. The chants, long hymns of endless
repetition and monotony, were well enough, perhaps;
the fire that was kept burning perpetually was a
fitting emblem of the sleepless wisdom and activity of
the Supreme Being in overcoming darkness with light.
But the boundless intoxication into which the priests
threw themselves by the excessive drinking of the
Haoma, the wild and irregular acts of frenzy by which
they expressed their religious fervour when under the
influence of the subtle drink, were adjuncts to the
simple purity of the bloodless sacrifice which disgusted
the king, and he hesitated long as to some reform in
these matters. The oldest Mazdayashnians declared
that the drinking of Haoma was an act, at once pleasing
to God and necessary to stimulate the zeal of the
priests in the long and monotonous chanting, which
would otherwise soon sink to a mere perfunctory performance of a wearisome task. The very repetition
which the hymns contained seemed to prove that they
were not intended to be recited by men not under
some extraordinary influence. Only the wild madness
of the Haoma drinker could sustain such an endless series
of repeated prayers with fitting devotion and energy.

All this the king heard and was not satisfied. He
attended the ceremonies with becoming regularity and
sat through the performance of the rites with exemplary
patience. But he was disgusted, and he desired a
reform. Then he remembered how Zoroaster himself
was a good Mazdayashnian, and how he had occupied

himself with religious studies from his youth up, and
how he had enjoyed the advantage of being the companion of Daniel, the Hebrew governor, whose grand
simplicity of faith had descended, to some degree, upon
his pupil.   The Hebrews, Darius knew, were a sober
people of the strongest religious convictions, and he
had heard that, although eating formed, in some way,
a part of their ceremonies, there was no intoxication
connected with their worship.   Zoroaster, he thought,
would be able to give him advice upon this point,
which would be good.   In sending for the man he
would fulfil the double purpose of seeming to grant
the queen's request, and at the same time, of providing
himself with a sage counsellor in his difficulties.   With
his usual impetuosity, he at once fulfilled his purpose,
assuring himself that Zoroaster must have forgotten
Nehushta by this time, and that he, the king, was
strong enough to prevent trouble if he had not.

But many days passed, and though the proclamation
was sent to all parts of the kingdom, nothing was
heard of Zoroaster.   His retreat was a sure one and
there was no possibility of his being found.

Atossa, who in her heart longed for Zoroaster's
return, both because by his means she hoped to bring
trouble upon Nehushta, and because she still felt something akin to love for him, began to fear that he might
be dead, or might have wandered out of the kingdom;
but Nehushta herself knew not whether to hope that
he would return, or to rejoice that she was to escape
the ordeal of meeting him.   She would have given
anything to see him for a moment, to decide, as it
were, whether she wished to see him, or not.   She
was deeply disturbed by the anxiety she felt and
longed to know definitely what she was to expect.

She began to hate Stakhar with its splendid gardens and gorgeous colonnades, with its soft southern air that blew across the valley of roses all day long, wafting up a wondrous perfume to the south windows. She hated the indolent pomp in which she lived and the idle luxury of her days. Something in her hot-blooded Hebrew nature craved for the blazing sun and the sand-wastes of Syria, for the breath of the desert and for the burning heat of the wilderness. She had scarcely ever seen these things, for she had sojourned during the one-and-twenty years of her life, in the most magnificent palaces of the kingdom, and amid the fairest gardens the hand of man could plant. But the love of the sun and of the sand was bred in the blood. She began to hate the soft cushions and the delicate silks and the endless flowers scenting the heavy air.

Stakhar[1] itself was a mighty fortress, in the valley of the Araxes, rising dark and forbidding from the banks of the little river, crowned with towers and turrets and massive battlements, that overlooked the fertile extent of gardens, as a stern schoolmaster frowning over a crowd of fair young children. But Darius had chosen the site of his palace at some distance from the stronghold; where the river bent suddenly round a spur of the mountain, and watered a wider extent of land. The spur of the hill ran down, by an easy gradation, into the valley; and beyond 'it the hills separated into the wide plain of Merodasht that stretched southward many farsangs to the southern pass. Upon this promontory the king had caused to be built a huge platform which was ascended by the broadest flight of steps in the whole world, so easy of

---

[1] Istakhar, called since the conquest of Alexander, Persepolis.

gradation that a man might easily have ridden up and then down again without danger to his horse. Upon the platform was raised the palace, a mighty structure resting on the vast columned porticoes and halls, built entirely of polished black marble, that contrasted strangely with the green slopes of the hills above and with the bright colours of the rose-gardens. Endless buildings rose behind the palace, and stretched far down towards the river below it. Most prominent of those above was the great temple of Auramazda, where the ceremonies were performed which gave Darius so much anxiety. It was a massive, square building, lower than the palace, consisting of stone walls surrounded by a deep portico of polished columns. It was not visible from the great staircase, being placed immediately behind the palace and hidden by it.

The walls and the cornices and the capitals of the pillars were richly sculptured with sacrificial processions, and long trains of soldiers and captives, with great inscriptions of wedge-shaped letters, and with animals of all sorts. The work was executed by Egyptian captives; and so carefully was the hard black marble carved and polished, that a man could see his face in the even surfaces, and they sent back the light like dark mirrors.

The valley above Stakhar was grand in its great outlines of crags and sharp, dark peaks, and the beetling fortress upon its rocky base, far up the gorge, seemed only a jutting fragment of the great mountain, thrown off and separated from the main chain by an earthquake, or some vast accident of nature. But from the palace itself the contrast of the views was great. On one side, the rugged hills, crag-crowned and bristling black against the north-western sky;

on the other, the great bed of rose-gardens and
orangeries and cultivated enclosures filled the plain,
till in the dim distance rose the level line of the soft
blue southern hills, blending mistily in the lazy light
of a far-off warmth.   It seemed as though on one side
of the palace were winter, and on the other summer;
on the one side cold, and on the other heat; on the
one side rough strength, and on the other gentle rest.

But Nehushta gazed northward and was weary of
the cold, and southward, and she wearied of the heat.
There was nothing—nothing in it all that was worth
one moment of the old sweet moonlit evenings among
the myrtles at Ecbatana.   When she thought, there
was nothing of all her royal state and luxury that
she would not readily give to have had Zoroaster remain faithful to her.   She had put him away from
her heart, driven him out utterly, as she believed;
but now that he was spoken of again, she knew not
whether she loved him a little in spite of all his
unfaithfulness, or whether it was only the memory of
the love she had felt before which stirred in her breast,
and made her unconsciously speak his name when she
was alone.

She looked back over the three years that were
passed, and she knew that she had done her duty by
the king.   She knew also that she had done it willingly, and that there had been many moments when
she said to herself that she loved Darius dearly.
Indeed, it was not hard to find a reason for loving
him, for he was brave and honest and noble in all his
thoughts and ways; and whatever he had been able
to do to show his love for Nehushta, he had done.
It was not the least of the things that had made her
life pass so easily, that she felt daily how she was

loved before her rival, and how, in her inmost heart, Atossa chafed at seeing Darius forsake her society for that of the Hebrew princess. If the king had wearied of her, Nehushta would very likely have escaped from the palace, and gone out to face any misfortunes the world might hold for her, rather than remain to bear the scoffing of the fair smiling woman she so hated. Or, she would have stolen in by night to where Atossa slept, and the wicked-looking Indian knife she wore, would have gone down, swift and sure, to the very haft, into the queen's heart. She would not have borne tamely any slight upon her beauty or her claims. But, as it was, she reigned supreme. The king was just, and showed no difference in the state and attendance of the two queens, but it was to Nehushta he turned, when he drank deep at the banquet and pledged the loving cup. It was to Nehushta that he went when the cares of state were heavy and he needed counsel; and it was upon her lap he laid his weary head, when he had ridden far and fast for many days, returning from some hard-fought field.

But the queens hated each other with a fierce hatred, and when Darius was absent, their divisions broke out sometimes into something like open strife. Their guards buffeted each other in the courts, and their slave-women tore out each other's hair upon the stairways. Then, when the king returned, there reigned an armed peace for a time, which none dared break. But rumours of the disturbances that had taken place often reached the royal ears, and Darius was angry and swore great oaths, but could do nothing; being no wiser than many great men who have had to choose between the caprices of two women who hated each other.

Now the rumour went abroad that Zoroaster would return to the court; and for a space, the two queens kept aloof, for both knew that if he came back, some mortal conflict would of necessity arise between them; and each watched the other, and was cautious.

The days passed by, but no one answered the proclamation. No one had seen or heard of Zoroaster, since the night when he left the palace at Shushan. He had taken nothing with him, and had left no trace behind to guide the search. Many said he had left the kingdom; some said he was dead in the wilderness. But Nehushta sighed and took little rest, for do what she would, she had hoped to see him once more.

CHAPTER XV.

THE interior of the temple was lighted with innumerable lamps, suspended from the ceiling, of bronze and of the simplest workmanship, like everything which pertained to the worship of Auramazda. In the midst, upon a small altar of black stone, stood a bronze brazier, shaped like a goblet, wherein a small fire of wood burned quietly, sending up little wreaths of smoke, which spread over the flat ceiling and hung like a mist about the lamps; before the altar lay a supply of fuel—fine, evenly-cut sticks of white pinewood, piled in regular order in a symmetrical heap. At one extremity of the oblong hall stood a huge mortar of black marble, having a heavy wooden pestle, and standing upon a circular base, in which was cut a channel all around, with an opening in the front from which the Haoma juice poured out abundantly when the fresh milkweed was moistened and pounded together in the mortar. A square receptacle of marble received the fluid, which remained until it had fermented during several days, and had acquired the intoxicating strength for which it was prized, and to which it owed its sacred character. By the side of this vessel, upon a low marble table, lay a huge wooden ladle; and two golden cups, short and wide, but made smaller in the middle like a sand-glass, stood there also.

At the opposite end of the temple, before a marble screen which shielded the doorway, was placed a great carved chair of ebony and gold and silver, raised upon a step above the level of the floor.

It was already dark when the king entered the temple, dressed in his robes of state, with his sword by his side, his long sceptre tipped with the royal sphere in his right hand, and the many-pointed crown upon his head. His heavy black beard had grown longer in the three years that had passed, and flowed down over his vest of purple and white halfway to his belt. His face was stern, and the deep lines of his strong features had grown more massive in outline. With the pride of every successive triumph had come also something more of repose and conscious power. His step was slower, and his broad brown hand grasped the golden sceptre with less of nervous energy and more unrelenting force. But his brows were bent, and his expression, as he took his seat before the screen, over against the altar of the fire, was that of a man who was prepared to be discontented and cared little to conceal what he felt.

After him came the chief priest, completely robed in white, with a thick, white linen sash rolled for a girdle about his waist, the fringed ends hanging stiffly down upon one side. Upon his head he wore a great mitre, also of white linen, and a broad fringed stole of the same material fell in two wide bands from each side of his neck to his feet. His beard was black and glossy, fine as silk, and reached almost to his waist. He came and stood with his back to the king and his face to the altar, ten paces from the second fire.

Then, from behind the screen and from each side of it, the other priests filed out, two and two, all clad in white like the chief priest, save that their mitres were smaller and they wore no stole. They came out and ranged themselves around the walls of the temple, threescore and nine men, of holy order, trained in the ancient chanting of the Mazdayashnian hymns; men in the prime and strength of life, black-bearded and broad-shouldered, whose massive brows and straight features indicated noble powers of mind and body.

The two who stood nearest to the chief priest came forward, and taking from his hands a square linen cloth he bore, bound it across his mouth and tied it behind his neck in a firm knot by means of strings. Then, one of them put into his left hand a fan of eagles' feathers, and the other gave him a pair of wrought-iron pincers. Then they left him to advance alone to the altar.

He went forward till he was close to the bronze brazier, and stooping down, he took from the heap of fuel a clean white stick, with the pincers, which he carefully laid upon the fire. Then with his left hand he gently fanned the flames, and his mouth being protected by the linen cloth in such a manner that his breath could not defile the sacred fire, he began slowly and in a voice muffled by the bandage he wore, to recite the beginning of the sacrificial hymn:

" *Best of all goods is purity.*
Glory, glory to him
Who is best and purest in purity.
For he who ruleth from purity, he abideth according
*   to the will of the Lord.*
The All-Wise giveth gifts for the works which man
*   doeth in the world for the Lord.*
He who protecteth the poor giveth the kingdom to
*   Ahura.*"[1]

[1] Probably the oldest hymns in the Avesta language.

Then all the priests repeated the verses together in chorus, their voices sounding in a unison which, though not precisely song, seemed tending to a musical cadence as the tones rose and fell again upon the last two syllables of each verse. And then again, the chief priest and the other priests together repeated the hymn, many times, in louder and louder chorus, with more and more force of intonation; till the chief priest stepped back from the fire, and delivering up the pincers and the fan, allowed the two assistants to unbind the cloth from his mouth.

He walked slowly up the temple on the left side, and keeping his right hand toward the altar, he walked seven times around it, repeating a hymn alone in low tones; till, after the seventh time, he went up to the farther end of the hall, and stood before the black marble trough in which the fermented Haoma stood ready, having been prepared with due ceremony three days before.

Then, in a loud voice, he intoned the chant in praise of Zaothra and Bareshma, holding high in his right hand the bundle of sacred stalks; which he, from time to time, moistened a little in the water from a vessel which stood ready, and sprinkled to the four corners of the temple. The priests again took up the strain in chorus, repeating over and over the burden of the song.

" *Zaothra, I praise thee and desire thee with praise !*
Bareshma, I praise thee and desire thee with praise !
Zaothra, with Bareshma united, I praise you and
*   desire you with praise !*
Bareshma, with Zaothra united, I praise you and
*   desire you with praise !*"

Suddenly the chief priest laid down the Bareshma,

and seizing one of the golden goblets, filled it, with the wooden ladle, from the dark receptacle of the juice. As he poured it high, the yellow light of the lamp caught the transparent greenish fluid, and made it sparkle strangely. He put the goblet to his lips and drank.

The king, sitting in silence upon his carved throne at the other extremity of the temple, bent his brows in a dark frown as he saw the hated ceremony begin. He knew how it ended, and grand as the words were which they would recite when the subtle fluid had fired their veins, he loathed to see the intoxication that got possession of them; and the frenzy with which they howled the sacred strains seemed to him to destroy the solemnity and dignity of a hymn, in which all that was solemn and high would otherwise have seemed to be united.

The chief priest drank and then, filling both goblets, gave them to the priests at his right and left hand; who, after drinking, passed each other, and made way for those next them; and so the whole number filed past the Haoma vessel and drank their share till they all had changed places, and those who had stood upon the right, now stood upon the left; and those who were first upon the left hand, were now upon the right. And when all had drunk, the chief priest intoned the great hymn of praise, and all· the chorus united with him in high, clear tones:

" *The All-Wise Creator, Ahura Mazda, the greatest, the best, the most fair in glory and majesty,*

" *The mightiest in his strength, the wisest in his wisdom, the holiest in his holiness, whose power is of all power the fairest,*

" *Who is very wise, who maketh all things to rejoice afar,*

" *Who hath made us and formed us, who hath saved us, the holiest among the heavenly ones,*

" *Him I adore and praise, unto him I declare the sacrifice, him I invite,*

" *I declare the sacrifice to the Protector, the Peace-maker, who maketh the fire to burn, who preserveth the wealth of the earth; the whole earth and the wisdom thereof, the seas and the waters, the land and all growing things, I invite to the sacrifice.*

" *Cattle and living things, and the fire of Ahura, the sure helper, the lord of the archangels,*

" *The nights and the days, I call upon, the purity of all created light,*

" *The Lord of light, the sun in his glory, glorious in name and worthy of honour,*

" *Who giveth food unto men, and multiplieth the cattle upon the earth, who causeth mankind to increase, I call upon and invite to the sacrifice,*

" *Water, and the centre of all waters, given and made of God, that refresheth all things and maketh all things to grow, I call upon and invite.*

" *The souls of the righteous and pure, the whole multitude of living men and women upon earth, I call upon and invite.*

" *I call upon the triumph and the mighty strength of God,*

" *I call upon the archangels who keep the world, upon the months, upon the pure, new moon, the lordship of purity in heaven,*

" *I call upon the feasts of the years and the seasons, upon the years and the months and days,*

" *I call upon the star Ahura,[1] and upon the one great*

---

[1] Ahura, Jupiter. Tistrya, Sirius.

and eternal in purity, and upon all the stars, the works of God,

" Upon the star Tistrya I call, the far-shining, the magnificent—upon the fair moon that shineth upon the young cattle, upon the glorious sun swift in the race of his flight, the eye of the Lord.

" I call upon the spirits and souls of the righteous, on the fire-begotten of the Lord, and upon all fires.

" Mountains and all hills, lightened and full of light.

" Majesty of kingly honour, the Majesty of the king which dieth not, is not diminished,

" All wisdom and blessings and true promises, all men who are full of strength and power and might,

" All places and lands and countries beneath the heavens, and above the heavens, light without beginning, existing, and without end,

" All creatures pure and good, male and female upon the earth.

" All you I invite and call upon to the sacrifice.

" Havani, pure, lord of purity !

" Shavanghi, pure, lord of purity !

" Rapithwina, pure, lord of purity !

" Uzayéirina, pure, lord of purity !

" Aiwishruthrema, Aibigaya, pure, lord of purity !

" Ushahina, pure, lord of purity !

" To Havani, Shavanghi and Vishya, the pure, the lords of purity most glorious, be honour and prayer and fulfilment and praise.

" To the days, and the nights, and the hours, the months and the years and the feasts of years, be honour and prayer and fulfilment and praise before Auramazda, the All-Wise, for ever and ever and ever." [1]

---

[1] Partly a translation, partly a close imitation in a condensed form of Yashna I.

As the white-robed priests shouted the verses of the long hymn, their eyes flashed and their bodies moved rhythmically from side to side with an ever-increasing motion. From time to time, the golden goblets were filled with the sweet Haoma juice, and passed rapidly from hand to hand along the line, and as each priest drank more freely of the subtle fermented liquor, his eyes gained a new and more unnatural light, and his gestures grew more wild, while the whole body of voices rose together from an even and dignified chant to an indistinguishable discord of deafening yells.

Ever more and more they drank, repeating the verses of the hymn without order or sequence. One man repeated a verse over and over again in ear-piercing shrieks, swaying his body to and fro till he dropped forward upon the ground, foaming at the mouth, his features distorted with a wild convulsion, and his limbs as rigid as stone. Here, a band of five locked their arms together, and, back to back, whirled madly round, screaming out the names of the archangels, in an indiscriminate rage of sound and broken syllables. One, less enduring than the rest, relaxed his hold upon his fellow's arm and fell headlong on the pavement, while the remaining four were carried on by the force of their whirling, and fell together against others who steadied themselves against the wall, swaying their heads and arms from side to side. Overthrown by the fall of their companions, these in their turn fell forward upon the others, and in a few moments, the whole company of priests lay grovelling one upon the other, foaming at the mouth, but still howling out detached verses of their hymn—a mass of raging, convulsed humanity, tearing each other in the frenzy of drunkenness, rolling over and over each other in the twisted contortions of frenzied maniacs. The air grew thick with the smoke of the fire and of the lamps, and the unceasing, indescribable din of the hoarsely howling voices seemed to make the very roof rock upon the pillars that held it up, as though the stones themselves must go mad and shriek in the universal fury of sound. The golden goblets rolled upon the marble pavement, and the sweet green juice ran in slimy streams upon the floor. The high priest himself, utterly intoxicated and screaming with a voice like a wild beast in agony, fell backwards across the marble vase at the foot of the mortar and his hand and arm plashed into the dregs of the fermented Haoma.

Never had the drunken frenzy reached such a point before. The king had sat motionless and frowning upon his seat until he saw the high priest fall head-long into the receptacle of the sacred Haoma. Then, with a groan, he laid his two hands upon the arms of his carved chair, and rose to his feet in utter disgust and horror. But, as he turned to go, he stood still and shook from head to foot, for he saw beside him a figure that might, at such a moment, have startled the boldest.

A tall man of unearthly looks stood there, whose features he seemed to know, but could not recognise. His face was thin to emaciation, and his long, white hair fell in tangled masses, with his huge beard, upon his half-naked shoulders and bare chest. The torn, dark mantle he wore was falling to the ground as he faced the drunken herd of howling priests and lifted up his thin blanched arms and bony fingers, as though in protest at the hideous sight. His deep-set eyes were blue and fiery, flashing with a strange light. He seemed not to see Darius, but he gazed in deepest

horror upon the writhing mass of bestial humanity
below.

Suddenly his arms shook, and standing there, against
the dark marble screen, like the very figure and incarnation of fate, he spoke in a voice that, without effort,
seemed to dominate the hideous din of yelling voices—
a voice that was calm and clear as a crystal bell, but
having that in it which carried instantly the words he
spoke to the ears of the very most besotted wretch that
lay among the heaps upon the floor—a voice that
struck like a sharp steel blade upon iron.

"I am the prophet of the Lord. Hold ye your
peace."

As a wild beast's howling suddenly diminishes and
grows less and dies away to silence, when the hunter's
arrow has sped close to the heart with a mortal wound,
so in one moment, the incoherent din sank down, and
the dead stillness that followed was dreadful by contrast. Darius stood with his hand upon the arm of
his chair, not understanding the words of the fearful
stranger; still less the mastering power those words
had upon the drunken priests. But his courage did
not desert him, and he feared not to speak.

"How sayest thou that thou art a prophet? Who
art thou?" he asked.

"Thou knowest me and hast sent for me," answered
the white-haired man, in his calm tones; but his fiery
eyes rested on the king's, and Darius almost quailed
under the glance. "I am Zoroaster; I am come to
proclaim the truth to thee and to these miserable men,
thy priests."

The fear they felt had restored the frenzied men to
their senses. One by one, they rose and crept back
towards the high priest himself, who had struggled to

his feet, and stood upon the basement of the mortar above all the rest.

Then Darius looked, and he knew that it was Zoroaster, but he knew not the strange look upon his face, and the light in his eyes was not as the light of other days. He turned to the priests.

"Ye are unworthy priests," he cried angrily, "for ye are drunk with your own sacrifice, and ye defile God's temple with unseemly cries. Behold this man— can ye tell me whether he be indeed a prophet?" Darius, whose anger was fast taking the place of the awe he had felt when he first saw Zoroaster beside him, strode a step forward, with his hand upon his sword-hilt, as though he would take summary vengeance upon the desecrators of the temple.

"He is surely a liar!" cried the high priest from his position beyond the altar, as though hurling defiance at Zoroaster through the flames.

"He is surely a liar!" repeated all the priests together, following their head.

"He is a Magian, a worshipper of idols, a liar and the father of lies! Down with him! Slay him before the altar; destroy the unbeliever that entereth the temple of Ahura Mazda!"

"Down with the Magian! Down with the idolater!" cried the priests, and moved forward in a body toward the thin white-haired man who stood facing them, serene and high.

Darius drew his short sword and rushed before Zoroaster to strike down the foremost of the priests. But Zoroaster seized the keen blade in the air as though it had been a reed, and wrenched it from the king's strong grip, and broke it in pieces like glass, and cast the fragments at his feet. Darius staggered back in amazement, and the herd of angry men, in whose eyes still blazed the drunkenness of the Haoma, huddled together for a moment like frightened sheep.

"I have no need of swords," said Zoroaster, in his cold, clear voice.

Then the high priest cried aloud, and ran forward and seized a brand from the sacred fire.

"It is Angramainyus, the Power of Evil," he yelled fiercely. "He is come to fight with Auramazda in his temple! But the fire of the Lord shall destroy him!"

As the priest rushed upon him, with the blazing brand raised high to strike, Zoroaster faced him and fixed his eyes upon the angry man. The priest suddenly stood still, his hand in mid-air, and the stout piece of burning wood fell to the floor, and lay smouldering and smoking upon the pavement.

"Tempt not the All-Wise Lord, lest he destroy thee," said Zoroaster solemnly. "Hearken, ye priests, and obey the word from heaven. Take the brazier from your altar, and scatter the embers upon the floor, for the fire is defiled."

Silent and trembling, the priests obeyed, for they were afraid; but the high priest stood looking in amazement upon Zoroaster.

When the brazier was gone, and the coals were scattered out upon the pavement, and the priests had trodden out the fire with their leathern shoes, Zoroaster went to the black marble altar, and faced the east, looking towards the stone mortar at the end. He laid his long, thin hands upon the flat surface and drew them slowly together; and, in the sight of the priests, a light sprang up softly between his fingers; gradually at first, then higher and higher, till it stood like a blazing spear-head in the midst, emitting a calm, white

effulgence that darkened the lamps overhead, and shed
an unearthly whiteness on Zoroaster's white face.

He stepped back from the altar, and a low murmur
of astonishment rose from all the crowd of white-robed
men.   Darius stood in silent wonder, gazing alternately
upon the figure of Zoroaster, and upon the fragments
of his good sword that lay scattered upon the pavement.

Zoroaster looked round upon the faces of the priests
with blazing eyes :

" If ye be true priests of Ahura Mazda, raise with
me the hymn of praise," he said.   " Let it be heard in
the heavens, and let it echo beyond the spheres !"

Then his voice rose calm and clear above all the
others, and lifting up his eyes and hands, he intoned
the solemn chant:

" *He, who by truth ruleth in purity, abideth according
to the will of the Lord.*

" *The Lord All-Wise is the giver of gifts to men for
the works which men in the world shall do in the truth
of the Lord.*

" *He who protecteth the poor giveth the kingdom to
God.*

" *Best of all earthly goods is truth.*

" *Glory, glory on high for ever to him who is best in
heaven, and truest in truth on earth!* "

Zoroaster's grand voice rang out, and all the priests
sang melodiously together ; and upon the place which
had been the scene of such frenzy and fury and drunkenness, there descended a peace as holy and calm as the
quiet flame that burned without fuel upon the black
stone in the midst.   One by one, the priests came and
fell at Zoroaster's feet ; the chief priest first of all.

" Thou art the prophet and priest of the Lord," each

said, one after another. " I acknowledge thee to be
the chief priest, and I swear to be a true priest with
thee."

And last of all, the king, who had stood silently by,
came and would have kneeled before Zoroaster.   But
Zoroaster took his hands, and they embraced.

"Forgive me the wrong I did thee, Zoroaster," said
Darius.   "For thou art a holy man, and I will honour
thee as thou wast not honoured before."

"Thou hast done me no wrong," answered Zoroaster.
"Thou hast sent for me, and I am come to be thy
faithful friend, as I swore to thee, long ago, in the tent
at Shushan."

Then they took Zoroaster's torn clothes, and they
clad him in white robes and set a spotless mitre upon
his head ; and the king, for the second time, took his
golden chain from his own neck, and put it about
Zoroaster's shoulders.   And they led him away into
the palace.

CHAPTER XVI.

WHEN it was known that Zoroaster had returned, there was some stir in the palace. The news that he was made high priest soon reached Nehushta's ears, and she wondered what change had come over him in three years that could have made a priest of such a man. She remembered him young and marvellously fair, a warrior at all points, though at the same time an accomplished courtier. She could not imagine him invested with the robes of priesthood, leading a chorus of singers in the chanting of the hymns.

But it was not only as a chief priest that Darius had reinstalled Zoroaster in the palace. The king needed a counsellor and adviser, and the learned priest seemed a person fitted for the post.

On the following day, Nehushta, as was her wont, went out, in the cool of the evening, to walk in the gardens, attended by her maidens, her fan-girls and the slaves who bore her carpet and cushions in case she wished to sit down. She walked languidly, as though she hardly cared to lift her delicate slippered feet from the smooth walk, and often she paused and plucked a flower, and all her train of serving-women stopped behind her, not daring even to whisper among themselves, for the young queen was in no gentle humour of mind. Her face was pale and her eyes were heavy, for she knew the man she had so loved in other days was near, and though he had so bitterly deceived her, the sound of his sweet promises was yet in her ears; and sometimes, in her dreams, she felt the gentle breath of his mouth upon her sleeping lips, and woke with a start of joy that was but the forerunner of a new sadness.

Slowly she paced the walks of the rose-gardens, thinking of another place in the far north, where there had been roses, and myrtles too, upon a terrace where the moonlight was very fair.

As she turned a sharp corner where the overhanging shrubbery darkened the declining light to a dusky shade, she found herself face to face with the man of whom she was thinking. His tall thin figure, clad in spotless white robes, seemed like a shadow in the gloom, and his snowy beard and hair made a strange halo about his young face, that was so thin and worn. He walked slowly, his hands folded together, and his eyes upon the ground; while a few paces behind him two young priests followed with measured steps, conversing in low tones, as though fearing to disturb the meditations of their master.

Nehushta started a little and would have passed on, although she recognised the face of him she had loved. But Zoroaster lifted his eyes, and looked on her with so strange an expression that she stopped short in the way. The deep, calm light in his eyes awed her, and there was something in his majestic presence that seemed of another world.

"Hail, Nehushta!" said the high priest quietly.

But, at the sound of his voice, the spell was broken. The Hebrew woman lifted her head proudly, and her black eyes flashed again.

P

"Greet me not," she answered, "for the greeting of a liar is like the sting of the serpent that striketh unawares in the dark."

Zoroaster's face never changed, only his luminous eyes gazed on hers intently, and she paused again, as though riveted to the spot.

"I lie not, nor have lied to thee ever," he answered calmly. "Go thou hence, ask her whom thou hatest, whether I have deceived thee. Farewell."

He turned his gaze from her and passed slowly on, looking down to the ground, his hands folded before him. He left her standing in the way, greatly troubled and not understanding his saying.

Had she not seen with her eyes how he held Atossa in his arms on that evil morning in Shushan? Had she not seen how, when he was sent away, he had written a letter to Atossa and no word to herself? Could these things which she had seen and known, be untrue? The thought was horrible—that her whole life had perhaps been wrecked and ruined by a mistake. And yet there was not any mistake, she repeated to herself. She had seen ; one must believe what one sees. She had heard Atossa's passionate words of love, and had seen Zoroaster's arms go round her drooping body ; one must believe what one sees and hears and knows !

But there was a ringing truth in his voice just now when he said : "I lie not, nor have lied to thee ever." A lie—no, not spoken, but done; and the lie of an action is greater than the lie of a word. And yet, his voice sounded true just now in the dusk, and there was something in it, something like the ring of a far regret. "Ask her whom thou hatest," he had said. That was Atossa. There was no other woman whom she hated —no man save him.

She had many times asked herself whether or no she loved the king. She felt something for him that she had not felt for Zoroaster. The passionate enthusiasm of the strong, dark warrior sometimes carried her away and raised her with it; she loved his manliness, his honesty, his unchanging constancy of purpose. And yet Zoroaster had had all these, and more also, though they had shown themselves in a different way. She looked back and remembered how calm he had always been, how utterly superior in his wisdom. He seemed scarcely mortal, until he had one day fallen— and fallen so desperately low in her view, that she loathed the memory of that feigned calmness and wisdom and purity. For it must have been feigned. How else could he have put his arms about Atossa, and taken her head upon his breast, while she sobbed out words of love?

But if he loved Atossa, she loved him as well. She said so, cried it aloud upon the terrace where any one might have heard it. Why then had he left the court, and hidden himself so long in the wilderness? Why, before going out on his wanderings, had he disguised himself, and gone and stood where the procession passed, and hissed out a bitter insult as Nehushta went by? For her sake he had abandoned his brilliant life these three years, to dwell in the desert, to grow so thin and miserable of aspect that he looked like an old man. And his hair and beard were white—she had heard that a man might turn white from sorrow in a day. Was it grief that had so changed him? Grief to see her wedded to the king before his eyes? His voice rang so true: "Ask her whom thou hatest," he had said. In truth she would ask. It was all too inexplicable, and the sudden thought that she had perhaps wronged him three long years ago—even the possibility of the thought that seemed so little possible to her yesterday—wrought strangely in her breast, and terrified her. She would ask Atossa to her face whether Zoroaster had loved her. She would tell how she had seen them together upon the balcony, and heard Atossa's quick, hot words. She would threaten to tell the king; and if the elder queen refused to answer truth, she would indeed tell him and put her rival to a bitter shame.

She walked more quickly upon the smooth path, and her hands wrung each other, and once she felt the haft of that wicked Indian knife she ever wore. When she turned back and went up the broad steps of the palace, the moon was rising above the far misty hills to eastward, and there were lights beneath the columned portico. She paused and looked back across the peaceful valley, and far down below, a solitary nightingale called out a few melancholy notes, and then burst forth into glorious song.

Nehushta turned again to go in, and there were tears in her dark eyes, that had not stood there for many a long day. But she clasped her hands together, and went forward between the crouching slaves, straight to Atossa's apartment. It was not usual for any one to gain access to the elder queen's inner chambers without first obtaining permission from Atossa herself, and Nehushta had never been there. They met rarely in public, and spoke little, though each maintained the appearances of courtesy; but Atossa's smile was the sweeter of the two. In private they never saw each other; and the queen's slaves would perhaps have tried to prevent Nehushta from entering, but her black eyes flashed upon them in such dire wrath as she saw them before her, that they crouched away and let her pass on unmolested.

Atossa sat, as ever at that hour, in her toilet-chamber, surrounded by her tirewomen. The room was larger than the one at Shushan, for she had caused it to be built after her own plans; but her table was the same as ever, and upon it stood the broad silver mirror, which she never allowed to be left behind when she travelled.

Her magnificent beauty had neither changed nor faded in three years. Such strength as hers was not to be broken, nor worn out, by the mere petty annoy-ances of palace life. She could sustain the constant little warfare she waged against the king, without even so much as looking careworn and pale for a moment, though the king himself often looked dark and weary, and his eyes were heavy with sleepless-ness for the trouble she gave him. Yet he could never determine to rid himself of her, even when he began to understand the profound badness of her character. She exercised a certain fascination over him, as a man grows fond of some beautiful, wicked beast he has half-tamed, though it turn and show its teeth at him sometimes, and be altogether more of a care than a pastime. She was so fair and evil that he could not hurt her; it would have seemed a crime to destroy anything so wondrously made. Moreover, she could amuse him and make many an hour pass pleasantly when she was so disposed.

She was fully attired for the banquet that was to take place late in the evening, but her women were still about her, and she looked at herself critically in the mirror, and would have changed the pinning of her tiara, so that her fair hair should fall forward upon one side, instead of backwards over her shoulder. She tried the effect of the change upon her face, and peered into the mirror beneath the bright light of the tall lamps; when, on a sudden, as she looked, she met the reflection of two angry dark eyes, and she knew that Nehushta was behind her.

She rose to her feet, turning quickly, and the sweep of her long robe overthrew the light carved chair upon the marble floor. She faced Nehushta with a cold smile that betrayed surprise at being thus interrupted in her toilet rather than any dread of the interview. Her delicate eyebrows arched themselves in something of scorn, but her voice came low and sweet as ever.

" It is rarely indeed that the queen Nehushta deigns to visit her servant," she said. " Had she sent warning of her coming, she would have been more fittingly received."

Nehushta stood still before her. She hated that cool, still voice that choked her like a tightening bowstring about her neck.

" We have small need of court formalities," answered the Hebrew woman, shortly. " I desire to speak with you alone upon a matter of importance."

" I am alone," returned Atossa, seating herself upon the carved chair, which one of the slaves had instantly set up again, and motioning to Nehushta to be seated. But Nehushta glanced at the serving-women and remained standing.

" You are not alone," she said briefly.

" They are not women—they are slaves," answered Atossa, with a smile.

" Will you not send them away?"

" Why should I?"

"You need not—I will," returned Nehushta. "Be-gone, and quickly!" she added, turning to the little group of women and slave-girls who stood together, looking on in wonder. At Nehushta's imperious com-mand, they hurried through the door, and the curtains fell behind them. They knew Nehushta's power in the palace too well to hesitate to obey her, even in the presence of their own mistress.

"Strange ways you have!" exclaimed Atossa, in a low voice. She was fiercely angry, but there was no change in her face. She dangled a little chain upon her finger, and tapped the ground with her foot as she sat. That was all.

"I am not come here to wrangle with you about your slaves. They will obey me without wrangling. I met Zoroaster in the gardens an hour since."

"By a previous arrangement, of course?" suggested Atossa, with a sneer. But her clear blue eyes fixed themselves upon Nehushta with a strange and deadly look.

"Hold your peace and listen to me," said Nehushta in a fierce, low voice, and her slender hand stole to the haft of the knife by her side.

Atossa was a brave woman, false though she was; but she saw that the Hebrew princess had her in her power—she saw the knife and she saw the gleam in those black eyes. They were riveted on her face, and she grew grave and remained silent.

"Tell me the truth," pursued Nehushta hurriedly. "Did Zoroaster love you three years ago—when I saw you in his arms upon the terrace the morning when he came back from Ecbatana?"

But she little knew the woman with whom she had to deal. Atossa had found time in that brief moment

to calculate her chances of safety. A weaker woman
would have lied; but the fair queen saw that the
moment had come wherein she could reap a rich harvest of vengeance upon her rival, and she trusted to
her coolness and strength to deliver her if Nehushta
actually drew the knife she wore.

"I loved him," she said slowly. "I love him yet,
and I hate you more than I love him. Do you understand?"

"Speak—go on!" cried Nehushta, half breathless
with anger.

"I loved him, and I hated you. I hate you still,"
repeated the queen slowly and gravely. "The letter
I had from him was written to you—but it was brought
to me. Nay—be not so angry, it was very long ago.
Of course you can murder me, if you please—you
have me in your power, and you are but a cowardly
Jew, like twenty of my slave-women. I fear you not.
Perhaps you would like to hear the end?"

Nehushta had come nearer and stood looking down
at the beautiful woman, her arms folded before her.
Atossa never stirred as Nehushta approached, but kept
her eye steadily fixed on hers. Nehushta's arms were
folded, and the knife hung below her girdle in its loose
sheath.

Atossa's white arm went suddenly out and laid hold
of the haft, and the keen blue steel flashed out of its
scabbard with a sheen like dark lightning on a summer's evening.

Nehushta started back as she saw the sharp weapon
in her enemy's hand. But Atossa laughed a low sweet
laugh of triumph.

"You shall hear the end now," she said, holding the
knife firmly in her hand. "You shall not escape

hearing the end now, and you shall not murder me
with your Indian poisoner here." She laughed again
as she glanced at the ugly curve of the dagger. " I
was talking with Zoroaster," she continued, " when I
saw you upon the stairs, and then—oh, it was so sweet !
I cried out that he should never leave me again, and I
threw my arms about his neck—his lordly neck that
you so loved !—and I fell, so that he had to hold me
up. And you saw him. Oh, it was sweet ! It was
the sweetest moment of my life when I heard you
groan and hurry away and leave us ! It was to hurt
you that I did it—that I humbled my queenliness
before him ; but I loved him, though—and he, he your
lover, whom you despised then and cast away for this
black-faced king of ours—he thrust me from him, and
pushed me off, and drove me weeping to my chamber ;
and he said he loved me not, nor wished my love. Ay,
that was bitter, for I was ashamed—I who never was
shamed of man or woman. But there was more sweetness in your torment than bitterness in my shame.
He never knew you were there. He screamed out to
you from the crowd in the procession his parting curse
on your unfaithfulness and went out—but he nearly
killed those two strong spearmen who tried to seize
him. How strong he was then, how brave ! What a
noble lover for any woman ! So tall and delicate and
fair with all his strength ! He never knew why you
left him—he thought it was to wear the king's purple,
to thrust a bit of gold in your hair ! He must have
suffered—you have suffered too—such delicious torture,
I have often soothed myself to sleep with the thought
of it. It is very sweet for me to see you lying there
with my wound in your heart. It will rankle long ;
you cannot get it out—you are married to the king

now, and Zoroaster has turned priest for love of you.
I think even the king would hardly love you if he
could see you now—you look so pale.   I will send for
the Chaldean physician—you might die.   I should be
sorry if you died, you could not suffer any more then.
I could not give up the pleasure of hurting you—you
have no idea how delicious it is.   Oh, how I hate you ! "

Atossa rose suddenly to her feet, with flashing eyes.
Nehushta, in sheer horror of such hideous cruelty, had
fallen back against the door-post, and stood grasping
the curtain with one hand while the other was pressed
to her heart, as though to control the desperate agony
she suffered.   Her face was paler than the dead, and
her long, black hair fell forward over her ghastly
cheeks.

" Shall I tell you more ? " Atossa began again.
" Should you like to hear more of the truth ?   I could
tell you how the king——"

But as she spoke, Nehushta threw up her hands and
pressed them to her throbbing temples ; and with a low
wail, she turned and fled through the doorway between
the thick curtains, that parted with her weight and
fell together again when she had passed.

" She will tell the king," said Atossa aloud, when
she was gone.   " I care not—but I will keep the
knife," she added, laying the keen blade upon the
table, amid the little instruments of her toilet.

But Nehushta ran fast through the corridors and
halls till she came to her slaves who had waited for
her at the entrance to the queen's apartment.   Then
she seemed to recollect herself, and slackened her pace,
and went on to her own chambers.   But her women
saw her pale face, and whispered together as they
cautiously followed her.

She was wretched beyond all words. In a moment, her doubts and her fears had all been realised, and the stain of unfaithfulness had been washed from the memory of her lover. But it was too late to repent her hastiness. She had been married to Darius now for nearly three years, and Zoroaster was a man so changed that she would hardly have recognised him that evening, had she not known that he was in the palace. He looked more like the aged Daniel whom he had buried at Ecbatana than like the lordly warrior of three years ago. She wondered, as she thought of the sound of his voice in the garden, how she could ever have doubted him, and the remembrance of his clear eyes was both bitter and sweet to her.

She lay upon her silken pillows and wept hot tears for him she had loved long ago, for him and for herself—most of all for the pain she had made him suffer, for that bitter agony that had turned his young, fair locks to snowy white; she wept the tears for him that she could fancy he must have shed in those long years for her. She buried her face and sobbed aloud, so that even the black fan-girl who stood waving the long palm-leaf over her in the dim light of the bedchamber —even the poor black creature from the farther desert, whom her mistress did not half believe human, felt pity for the royal sorrow she saw, and took one hand from the fan to brush the tears from her small red eyes.

Nehushta's heart was broken, and from that day none saw her smile. In one hour the whole misery of all possible miseries came upon her, and bowed her to the ground, and crushed out the life and the light of her nature. As she lay there, she longed to die, as she had never longed for anything while she lived, and

she would have had small hesitation in killing the
heart that beat with such agonising pain in her breast—
saving that one thought prevented her.   She cared not
for revenge any more.   What was the life of that cold,
cruel thing, the queen, worth, that by taking it, she
could gain comfort?   But she felt and knew that,
before she died, she must see Zoroaster once more, and
tell him that she knew all the truth—that she knew
he had not deceived her, and that she implored his
forgiveness for the wrong she had done him.   He
would let her rest her head upon his breast and weep
out her heartful of piteous sorrow once before she died.
And then—the quiet stream of the Araxes flowed softly,
cold and clear, among the rose-gardens below the palace.
The kindly water would take her to its bosom, beneath
the summer's moon, and the nightingales she loved
would sing her a gentle good-night—good-night for
ever, while the cool wave flowed over her weary breast
and aching head.

CHAPTER XVII.

On the next day, in the cool of the evening, Nehushta walked again in the garden. But Zoroaster was not there. And for several days Nehushta came at that hour, and at other hours in the day, but found him not. She saw him indeed from time to time in public, but she had no opportunity of speaking with him as she desired. At last, she determined to send for him, and to see whether he would come, or not.

She went out, attended only by two slaves; the one bearing a fan and the other a small carpet and a cushion—black women from the southern parts of Syria, towards Egypt, who would not understand the high Persian she would be likely to speak with Zoroaster, though her own Hebrew tongue was intelligible to them. When she reached a quiet spot, where one of the walks ended suddenly in a little circle among the rose-trees, far down from the palace, she had her carpet spread, and her cushion was placed upon it, and she wearily sat down. The fan-girl began to ply her palm-leaf, as much to cool the heated summer air as to drive away the swarms of tiny gnats which abounded in the garden. Nehushta rested upon one elbow, her feet drawn together upon the carpet of dark soft colours and waited a few minutes as though in thought. At last she seemed to have decided, and turned to the slave who had brought her cushion, as she stood at a little distance, motionless, her hands folded and hidden under the thickness of the broad sash that girded her tunic at the waist.

"Go thou," said the queen, "and seek out the high priest Zoroaster, and bring him hither quickly."

The black woman turned and ran like a deer down the narrow path, disappearing in a moment amongst the shrubbery.

The breeze of the swinging fan blew softly on Nehushta's pale face and stirred the locks of heavy hair that fell from her tiara about her shoulders. Her eyes were half closed as she leaned back, and her lips were parted in a weary look of weakness that was new to her. Nearly an hour passed and the sun sank low, but Nehushta hardly stirred from her position.

It seemed very long before she heard steps upon the walk—the quick soft step of the slave-woman running before, barefooted and fleet, and presently the heavier tread of a man's leather shoe. The slave stopped at the entrance to the little circle of rose-trees, and a moment later, Zoroaster strode forward, and stood still and made a deep obeisance, a few steps from Nehushta.

"Forgive me that I sent for thee, Zoroaster," said the queen in quiet tones. But, as she spoke, a slight blush overspread her face, and relieved her deadly pallor. "Forgive me—I have somewhat to say which thou must hear."

Zoroaster remained standing before her as she spoke, and his luminous eyes rested upon her quietly.

"I wronged thee three years ago, Zoroaster," said the queen in a low voice, but looking up at him. "I pray thee, forgive me—I knew not what I did."

"I forgave thee long ago," answered the high priest.

"I did thee a bitter wrong—but the wrong I did myself was even greater. I never knew till I went and asked—her!" At the thought of Atossa, the Hebrew woman's eyes flashed fire, and her small fingers clenched upon her palm. But, in an instant, her sad, weary look returned.

"That is all—if you forgive me," she said, and turned her head away. It seemed to her that there was nothing more to be said. He did not love her—he was far beyond love.

"Now, by Ahura Mazda, I have indeed forgiven thee. The blessing of the All-Wise be upon thee!" Zoroaster bent again, as though to take his leave, and he would have gone from her.

But when she heard his first footsteps, Nehushta raised herself a little and turned quickly towards him. It seemed as though the only light she knew were departing from her day.

"You loved me once," she said, and stopped, with an appealing look on her pale face. It was very weak of her; but oh! she was far spent with sorrow and grief. Zoroaster paused, and looked back upon her, very calmly, very gently.

"Ay—I loved you once—but not now. There is no more love in the earth for me. But I bless you for the love you gave me."

"I loved you so well," said Nehushta. "I love you still," she added, suddenly raising herself and gazing on him with a wild look in her eyes. "Oh, I love you still!" she cried passionately. "I thought I had put you away—forgotten you—trodden out your memory that I so hated I could not bear to hear your name! Ah! why did I do it; miserable woman that I am! I love you now—I love you—I love you with my whole heart—and it is too late !" She fell back upon her cushion, and covered her face with her hands, and her breast heaved with passionate, tearless sobbing.

Zoroaster stood still, and a deep melancholy came over his beautiful, ethereal face. No regret stirred his breast, no touch of the love that had been waked his heart that slept for ever in the peace of the higher life. He would not have changed from himself to the young lover of three years ago, if he had been able. But he stood calm and sorrowful, as an angel from heaven gazing on the grief of the world—his thoughts full of sympathy for the pains of men, his soul still breathing the painless peace of the outer firmament whence he had come and whither he would return.

"Nehushta," he said at last, seeing that her sobbing did not cease, "it is not meet that you should thus weep for anything that is past. Be comforted; the years of life are few, and you are one of the great ones of the earth. It is needful that all should suffer. Forget not that although your heart be heavy, you are a queen, and must bear yourself as a queen. Take your life strongly in your hands and live it. The end is not far and your peace is at hand."

Nehushta looked up suddenly and grew very grave as he spoke. Her heavy eyes rested on his, and she sighed—but the sigh was still broken by the trembling of her past sobs.

"You, who are a priest and a prophet," she said,— "you, who read the heaven as it were a book—tell me, Zoroaster, is it not far? Shall we meet beyond the stars, as you used to tell me—so long ago?"

"It is not far," he answered, and a gentle smile illuminated his pale face. "Take courage—for truly it is not far."

He gazed into her eyes for a moment, and it seemed as though some of that steadfast light penetrated into her soul, for as he turned and went his way among the roses, a look of peace descended on her tired face, and she fell back upon her cushion and closed her eyes, and let the breeze of the palm-fan play over her wan cheeks and through her heavy hair.

But Zoroaster returned into the palace, and he was very thoughtful. He had many duties to perform, besides the daily evening sacrifice in the temple, for Darius consulted him constantly upon many matters connected with the state; and on every occasion Zoroaster's keen foresight and knowledge of men found constant exercise in the development of the laws and statutes Darius was forming for his consolidated kingdom. First of all, the question of religion seemed to him of paramount importance; and here Zoroaster displayed all his great powers of organisation, as well as the true and just ideas he held upon the subject. Himself an ascetic mystic, he foresaw the danger to others of attempting to pursue the same course, or even of founding a system of mystical study. The object of mankind must be the welfare of mankind, and a set of priests who should shut themselves off from their fellow-men to pursue esoteric studies and to acquire knowledge beyond the reach of common humanity, must necessarily forget humanity itself in their effort to escape from it. The only possible scheme upon which a religion for the world could be based—especially for such a world as the empire of Darius—must be one where the broad principle of common good living stood foremost, and where the good of all humanity should be the good of each man's soul.

The vast influence of Zoroaster's name grew day by

day, as from the palace of Stakhar he sent forth priests
to the various provinces, full of his own ideas, bearing
with them a simple form of worship and a rigid rule
of life, which the iron laws of Darius began at once to
enforce to the letter.   The vast body of existing hymns,
of which many were by no means distinctly Mazdayashnian, were reduced to a limited number contain-
ing the best and purest; and the multifarious mass of
conflicting caste practices, partly imported from India,
and partly inherited by the pure Persians from the
Aryan home in Sogdiana, was simplified and reduced
to a plain rule.   The endless rules of purification were
cut down to simple measures of health; the varying
practices in regard to the disposal of the dead were all
done away with by a great royal edict commanding the
building of Dakhmas, or towers of death, all over the
kingdom; within which the dead were laid by persons
appointed for the purpose, and which were cleansed by
them, at stated intervals.   Severe measures were taken
to prevent the destruction of cattle, for there were
evident signs of the decrease of the beasts of the field
in consequence of the many internal wars that had
waged of late; and special laws were provided for
the safety of dogs, which were regarded, for all reasons,
as the most valuable companions of men in those times,
as a means of protection to the flocks in the wilderness,
and as the scavengers and cleansers of the great cities.
Human life was protected by the most rigorous laws,
and the utmost attention was given to providing for
the treatment of women of all classes.   It would have
been impossible to conceive a system better fitted to
develop the resources of a semi-pastoral country, to
preserve peace and to provide for the increasing wants
and the public health of a multiplying people.

As for the religious rites, they assumed a form and a character which made them seem like simplicity itself by the side of the former systems; and which, although somewhat complicated by the additions and alterations of a later and more superstitious generation, have still maintained the noble and honourable characteristics imparted to them by the great reformer and compiler of the Mazdayashnian religion.

The days flew quickly by, and Zoroaster's power grew apace. It was as though the whole court and kingdom had been but waiting for him to come and be the representative of wisdom and justice beside the conquering king, who had in so short a time reduced so many revolutions and fought so many fields in the consolidation of his empire. Zoroaster laid hold of all the existing difficulties with a master-hand. His years of retirement seemed to have given him the accumulated force of many men, and the effect of his wise measures was quickly felt in every quarter of the provinces; while his words went forth like fire in the mouths of the priests he sent from Stakhar. He had that strange and rare gift, whereby a man inspires in his followers the profoundest confidence and the greatest energy to the performance of his will. He would have overthrown a world had he found himself resisted and oppressed, but every one of his statutes and utterances was backed by the royal arms and enforced by decrees against which there was no appeal. In a few months his name was spoken wherever the Persian rule was felt, and spoken everywhere with a high reverence; in which there was no fear mixed, such as people felt when they mentioned the Great King, and added quickly: "May he live for ever!"

In a few months the reform was complete, and the

half-clad ascetic had risen by his own wisdom and by
the power of circumstances into the chiefest position
in all Persia. Loaded with dignities, treated as the
next to the Great King in all things, wearing the royal
chain of office over his white priest's robes, and sitting
at the right hand of Darius at the feast, Zoroaster
nevertheless excited no envy among the courtiers, nor
encroached in any way upon their privileges. The few
men whom Darius trusted were indeed rarely at Stakhar,—the princes who had conspired against Smerdis,
and Hydarnes and a few of the chief officers of the
army,—they were mostly in the various provinces, in
command of troops and fortresses, actively employed
in enforcing the measures the king was framing with
Zoroaster, and which were to work such great changes
in the destinies of the empire. But when any of the
princes or generals were summoned to the court by the
king and learned to know what manner of man this
Zoroaster was, they began to love him and to honour
him also, as all those did who were near him. And
they went away, saying that never king had so wise
and just a counsellor as he was, nor one so worthy of
trust in the smallest as in the greatest things.

But the two queens watched him, and watched his
growing power, with different feelings. Nehushta
scarcely ever spoke to him, but gazed at him from her
sad eyes when none saw her; pondering over his pro-
phecy that foretold the end so near at hand. She had
a pride in seeing her old lover the strongest in the
whole land, holding the destinies of the kingdom as in
a balance; and it was a secret consolation to her to
know that he had been faithful to her after all, and
that it was for her sake that he had withdrawn into
the desert and given himself to those meditations from

which he had only issued to enjoy the highest power. And as she looked at him, she saw how he was much changed, and it hardly seemed as though in his body he were the same man she had so loved. Only when he spoke, and she heard the even, musical tones of his commanding voice, she sometimes felt the blood rise to her cheeks with the longing to hear once more some word of tender love, such as he had been used to speak to her. But though he often looked at her and greeted her ever kindly, his quiet, luminous eyes changed not when they gazed on her, nor was there any warmer touch of colour in the waxen whiteness of his face. His youth was utterly gone, as the golden light had faded from his hair. He was not like an old man— he was hardly like a man at all; but rather like some beautiful, strange angel from another world, who moved among men and spoke with them, but was not of them. She seemed to look upon a memory, to love the shadow cast on earth by a being that was gone. But she loved the memory and the shadow well, and month by month, as she gazed, she grew more wan and weary.

It would not have been like Darius to take any notice of a trouble that did not present itself palpably before him and demand his attention. Nehushta scarcely ever spoke of Zoroaster, and when the king mentioned him to her, it was always in connection with affairs of state. She seemed cold and indifferent, and the hot-blooded soldier monarch no longer looked on Zoroaster as a possible rival. He had white hair —he was therefore an old man, out of all questions of love. But Darius was glad that the Hebrew queen never referred to former times, nor ever seemed to regret her old lover. Had he known of that night meeting in Atossa's toilet chamber, and of what Atossa

had said then, his fury would probably have had no
bounds.   But he never knew.   Nehushta was too
utterly broken-hearted by the blow she had received
to desire vengeance, and though she quietly scorned all
intercourse with the woman who had injured her, she
cared not to tell the king of the injury.   It was too
late.   Had she known of the cruel deception that had
been practised on her, one hour before she had married
Darius, Atossa would have been in her grave these
three years, and Nehushta would not have been queen.
But the king knew none of these things, and rejoiced
daily in the wisdom of his chief counsellor and in the
favour Auramazda had shown in sending him such a
man in his need.

Meanwhile, Atossa's hatred grew apace.   She saw
with anger that her power of tormenting Nehushta
was gone from her, that the spirit she had loved to
torture was broken beyond all sensibility, and that the
man who had scorned her love was grown greater than
she.   Against his wisdom and the king's activity, she
could do little, and her strength seemed to spend itself
in vain.   Darius laughed mercilessly at her cunning
objections to Zoroaster's reforms ; and Zoroaster himself
eyed her coldly, and passed her by in silence when they
met.

She bethought herself of some scheme whereby to
destroy Zoroaster's power by a sudden and violent
shock ; and for a time, she affected a more than usual
serenity of manner, and her smile was sweeter than
ever.   If it were possible, she thought, to attract the
king's attention and forces to some distant point, it
would not be a difficult matter to produce a sudden
rising or disturbance in Stakhar, situated as the place
was upon the very extreme border of the kingdom,

within a few hours' march across the hills from the
uncivilised desert country, which was infested at that
time with hostile and turbulent tribes. She had a
certain number of faithful retainers at her command
still, whom she could employ as emissaries in both
directions, and in spite of the scene that had taken
place at Shushan when Phraortes was brought to her
by the king, she knew she could still command his
services for a revolution. He was a Magian at heart,
and hated the existing monarchy. He was rich and
powerful, and unboundedly vain—he could easily be
prevailed upon to accept the principality of Media as
a reward for helping to destroy the Persian kingdom;
and indeed the matter had been discussed between him
and the queen long ago.

Atossa revolved her scheme in her mind most carefully for two whole months, and at last she resolved
to act. Eluding all vigilance of the king, and laughing to herself at the folly of Darius and Zoroaster in
allowing her such liberty, she succeeded without much
trouble in despatching a letter to Phraortes, inquiring
whether her affairs were now in such a prosperous
condition as to admit of their being extended.

On the other hand, she sent a black slave she owned,
with gifts, into the country of the barbarian tribes beyond the hills, to discover whether they could be easily
tempted. This man she bribed with the promise of
freedom and rich possessions, to undertake the danger-
ous mission. She knew him to be faithful, and able
to perform the part he was to play.

In less than two months Phraortes sent a reply,
wherein he stated that the queen's affairs were so prosperous that they might with safety be extended as she
desired, and that he was ready to undertake any im-

provements provided she sent him the necessary directions and instructions.

The slave returned from the land of the dwellers in
tents, with the information that they were numerous
as the sands of the sea, riding like the whirlwinds
across the desert, keen as a race of eagles for prey,
devouring as locusts spreading over a field of corn, and
greedy as jackals upon the track of a wounded antelope.
Nothing but the terror of the Great King's name
restrained them within their boundaries; which they
would leave at a moment's notice, as allies of any one
who would pay them. They dwelt mostly beyond the
desert to eastward in the low hill country; and they
shaved their beards and slept with their horses in their
tents. They were more horrible to look upon than the
devils of the mountains, and fiercer than wolves upon
the mountain paths.

Allowing for the imagery of her slave's account,
Atossa comprehended that the people described could
be easily excited to make a hostile descent upon the
southern part of the kingdom, and notably upon the
unprotected region about Stakhar, where the fortress
could afford shelter to a handful of troops and fugitives,
but could in no wise defend the whole of the fertile
district from a hostile incursion.

Atossa spent much time in calculating the distance
from the palace to the fortress, and she came to the
conclusion that a body of persons moving with some
encumbrance might easily reach the stronghold in half
a day. Her plan was a simple one, and easy of execution; though there was no limit to the evil results its
success might have upon the kingdom.

She intended that a revolution should break out in
Media, not under the leadership of Phraortes, lest she

herself should perish, having been already suspected of complicity with him. But a man could be found— some tool of her powerful agent, who could be readily induced to set himself up as a pretender to the princi- pality of the province, and he could easily be crushed at a later period by Phraortes, who would naturally furnish the money and supplies for the insurrection.

As soon as the news reached Stakhar, Darius would, in all probability, set out for Media in haste to arrive at the scene of the disturbance. He would probably leave Zoroaster behind to manage the affairs of state, which had centred in Stakhar during the last year and more. If, however, he took him with him, and left the court to follow on as far as Shushan, Atossa could easily cause an incursion of the barbarous tribes from the desert. The people of the south would find them- selves abandoned by the king, and would rise against him, and Atossa could easily seize the power. If Zoroaster remained behind, the best plan would be to let the barbarians take their own course and destroy him. Separated from any armed force of magnitude sufficient to cope with a sudden invasion, he would surely fall in the struggle, or take refuge in an igno- minious flight. With the boldness of her nature, Atossa trusted to circumstances to provide her with an easy escape for herself; and in the last instance, she trusted, as she had ever done, to her marvellous beauty to save her from harm. To her beauty alone she owed her escape from many a fit of murderous anger in the time of Cambyses, and to her beauty she owed her salvation when Darius found her at Shushan, the wife and accomplice of the impostor Smerdis. She might again save herself by that means, if by no other, should she, by any mischance, fall into the hands of the barbarians. But she was determined to overthrow Zoroaster, even if she had to destroy her husband's kingdom in the effort. It was a bold and simple plan, and she doubted not of being successful.

During the months while she was planning these things, she was very calm and placid; her eyes met Zoroaster's with a frank and friendly glance that would have disarmed one less completely convinced of her badness; and her smile never failed the king when he looked for it. She bore his jests with unfailing equanimity and gentleness, for she felt that she should not have to bear them long. Even to Nehushta she gave an occasional glance as though of hurt sympathy —a look that seemed to say to the world that she regretted the Hebrew queen's sullen temper and moody ways, so different from her own, but regarded them all the while as the outward manifestation of some sickness, for which she was to be pitied rather than blamed.

But, as the time sped, her heart grew more and more glad, for the end was at hand, and there was a smell of death in the air of the sweet rose-valley.

CHAPTER XVIII.

ONCE more the spring months had come, and the fields grew green and the trees put forth their leaves. Four years had passed since Daniel had died in Ecbatana, leaving his legacy of wisdom to Zoroaster; and almost a year had gone by since Zoroaster had returned to the court at Stakhar. The time had sped very swiftly, except for Nehushta, whose life was heavy with a great weariness and her eyes hollow with suffering sleeplessness. She was not always the same, saving that she was always unhappy. There were days when she was resigned to her lot and merely hoped that it would soon be over; and she wondered how it was that she did not slip out of the gardens at evening, and go and sink her care and her great sorrow in the cool waves of the Araxes, far down below. But then the thought came over her that she must see his face once more; and it was always once more, so that the last time never came. And again, there were days when she hoped all things, madly, indiscriminately, without sequence—the king might die, Zoroaster might again love her, all might be well. But the mood of a hope that is senseless is very fleet, and despair follows close in its footsteps. Nehushta grew each time more sad, as she grew more certain that for her there was no hope.

At least it seemed as though Atossa had given up

loving Zoroaster and thought no more of him than of
another.   Indeed Atossa seemed more anxious to please
the king than formerly, in proportion as Darius seemed
less easily pleased by her.   But over all, Zoroaster's
supremacy was felt in the palace, and though he was
never known to be angry with any one, he was more
feared than the fierce king himself, for his calm clear
eyes were hard to meet and the words that fell from
his lips had in them the ring of fate.   Moreover, he
was known and his power was dreaded from one end
of the kingdom to the other, and his name was like the
king's signet, which sealed all things, and there was no
appeal.

Upon a fair morning in the spring-time, when the
sun was shining outside upon the roses still wet with
dew, the king sat in an inner hall, half lying upon a
broad couch, on which the warm rays of the sun fell
through an upper window.   He was watching with
absorbed attention the tricks of an Indian juggler who
had lately arrived at the court, and whom he had
summoned that morning to amuse a leisure hour, for
when the king was not actively engaged in business,
or fighting, he loved some amusement, being of a restless temper and mind that needed constant occupation.

Atossa sat near him, upon a carved chair, turning
over and over in her fingers a string of pearls as she
gazed at the performances of the juggler.   Two spearmen, clad in blue and scarlet and gold, stood motionless
by the door, and Darius and Atossa watched the sleight-
handed Indian alone.

The man tossed a knife into the air and caught it,
then two, then three, increasing the number in rapid
succession till a score of bright blades made a shining
circle in the air as he quickly tossed them up and

passed them from hand to hand and tossed them again. Darius laughed at the man's skill, and looked up at the queen.

"You remind me of that fellow," said Darius.

"The king is very gracious to his handmaiden," answered Atossa, smiling, "I think I am less skilful, but more fair."

"You are fairer, it is true," returned the king; "but as for your skill, I know not. You seem always to be playing with knives, but you never wound yourself any more than he does."

The queen looked keenly at Darius, but her lips smiled gently. The thought crossed her mind that the king perhaps knew something of what had passed between her and Nehushta nearly a year before, with regard to a certain Indian dagger. The knives the juggler tossed in the air reminded her of it by their shape. But the king laughed gaily and she answered without hesitation:

"I would it were true, for then I could be not only the king's wife, but the king's juggler!"

"I meant not so," laughed Darius. "The two would hardly suit one another."

"And yet, I need more skill than this Indian fellow, to be the king's wife," answered the queen slowly.

"Said I not so?"

"Nay—but you meant not so," replied Atossa, looking down.

"What I say, I mean," he returned. "You need all the fairness of your face to conceal the evil in your heart, as this man needs all his skill in handling those sharp knives, that would cut off his fingers if, unawares, he touched the wrong edge of them."

"I conceal nothing," said the queen, with a light

laugh. "The king has a thousand eyes—how should I
conceal anything from him?"

"That is a question which I constantly ask myself,"
answered Darius. "And yet, I often think I know
your thoughts less well than those of the black girl
who fans you when you are hot, and whose attention
is honestly concentrated upon keeping the flies from
your face—or of yonder stolid spearmen at the door,
who watch us, and honestly wish they were kings and
queens, to lie all day upon a silken couch, and watch
the tricks of a paid conjurer."

As Darius spoke, the guards he glanced at turned
suddenly and faced each other, standing on each side
of the doorway, and brought their heavy spears to the
ground with a ringing noise. In a moment the tall,
thin figure of Zoroaster, in his white robes, appeared
between them. He stopped respectfully at the threshold, waiting for the king to notice him, for, in spite
of his power and high rank, he chose to maintain
rigidly the formalities of the court.

Darius made a sign and the juggler caught his whirling knives, one after the other, and thrust them into
his bag, and withdrew.

"Hail, Zoroaster!" said the king. "Come near and
sit beside me, and tell me your business."

Zoroaster came forward and made a salutation, but
he remained standing, as though the matter on which
he came were urgent.

"Hail, king, and live for ever!" he said. "I am a
bearer of evil news. A rider has come speeding from
Ecbatana, escaped from the confusion. Media has
revolted, and the king's guards are besieged within the
fortress of Ecbatana."

Darius sat upright upon the edge of his couch; the

CHAP. XVIII.] ZOROASTER.

knotted veins upon his temples swelled with sudden anger and his brow flushed darkly.

"Doubtless it is Phraortes who has set himself up as king," he said. Then, suddenly and fiercely, he turned upon Atossa. "Now is your hour come," he cried in uncontrollable anger. "You shall surely die this day, for you have done this, and the powers of evil shall have your soul, which is of them, and of none other."

Atossa, for the first time in her whole life, turned pale to the lips and trembled, for she already seemed to taste death in the air. But even then, her boldness did not desert her, and she rose to her feet with a stateliness and a calmness that almost awed the king's anger to silence.

"Slay me if thou wilt," she said in a low voice, but firmly. "I am innocent of this deed." The great lie fell from her lips with a calmness that a martyr might have envied. But Zoroaster stepped between her and the king. As he passed her, his clear, calm eyes met hers for a moment. He read in her face the fear of death, and he pitied her.

"Let the king hear me," he said. "It is not Phraortes who has headed the revolt, and it is told me that Phraortes has fled from Ecbatana. Let the king send forth his armies and subdue the rebels, and let this woman go; for the fear of death is upon her and it may be that she has not sinned in this matter. And if she have indeed sinned, will the king make war upon women, or redden his hands with the blood of his own wife?"

"You speak as a priest—I feel as a man," returned the king, savagely. "This woman has deserved death many times—let her die. So shall we be free of her."

" It is not lawful to do this thing," returned Zoroaster coldly, and his glance rested upon the angry face of Darius, as he spoke, and seemed to subdue his furious wrath. "The king cannot know whether she have deserved death or not, until he have the rebels of Ecbatana before him. Moreover, the blood of a woman is a perpetual shame to the man who has shed it."

The king seemed to waver, and Atossa, who watched him keenly, understood that the moment had come in which she might herself make an appeal to him. In the suddenness of the situation she had time to ask herself why Zoroaster, whom she had so bitterly injured, should intercede for her. She could not understand his nobility of soul, and she feared some trap, into which she should fall by and by. But, meanwhile, she chose to appeal to the king's mercy herself, lest she should feel that she owed her preservation wholly to Zoroaster. It was a bold thought, worthy of a woman of her strength, in a moment of supreme danger.

With a quick movement she tore the tiara from her head and let it fall upon the floor. The mass of her silken hair fell all about her like a vesture of gold, and she threw herself at the king's feet, embracing his knees with a passionate gesture of appeal. Her face was very pale, and the beauty of it seemed to grow by the unnatural lack of colour, while her soft blue eyes looked up into the king's face with such an expression of imploring supplication that he was fain to acknowledge to himself that she moved his heart, for she had never looked so fair before. She spoke no word, but held his knees, and as she gazed, two beautiful great tears rolled slowly from under her eyelids, and trembled upon her pale, soft cheeks, and her warm, quick breath went up to his face.

Darius tried to push her from him, but she would not go, and he was forced to look at her, and his anger melted, and he smiled somewhat grimly, though his brows were bent.

" Go to," he said, " I jested. It is impossible for a man to slay anything so beautiful as you."

Atossa's colour returned to her cheeks, and bending down, she kissed the king's knees and his hands, and her golden hair fell all about her and upon the king's lap. But Darius rose impatiently, and left her kneeling by the couch. He was already angry with himself for having forgiven her, and he hated his own weakness bitterly.

" I will myself go hence at once with the guards, and I will take half the force from the fortress of Stakhar and go to Shushan, and thence, with the army that is there, I will be in Ecbatana in a few days. And I will utterly crush out these rebels who speak lies and do not acknowledge me. Remain here, Zoroaster, and govern this province until I return in triumph."

Darius glanced once more at Atossa, who lay by the couch, half upon it and half upon the floor, seemingly dazed at what had occurred ; and then he turned upon his heel and strode out of the room between the two spearmen of the guard, who raised their weapons as he passed, and followed him with a quick, rhythmical tread down the broad corridor outside.

Zoroaster was left alone with the queen.

As soon as Darius was gone, Atossa rose to her feet, and with all possible calmness proceeded to re-arrange her disordered hair and to place her head-dress upon her head. Zoroaster stood and watched her ; her hand trembled a little, but she seemed otherwise unmoved by what had occurred. She glanced up at

him from under her eyelids as she stood with her head
bent down and her hands raised, to arrange her hair.

"Why did you beg the king to spare my life?" she
asked. "You, of all men, must wish me dead."

"I do not wish you dead," he answered coldly.
"You have yet much evil to do in the world, but it
will not be all evil. Neither did I need to intercede
for you. Your time is not come, and though the king's
hand were raised to strike you, it would not fall upon
you, for you are fated to accomplish many things."

"Do you not hate me, Zoroaster?"

It was one of the queen's chief characteristics that
she never attempted concealment when it could be of
no use, and in such cases affected an almost brutal
frankness. She almost laughed as she asked the question—it seemed so foolish, and yet she asked it.

"I do not hate you," answered the priest. "You
are beneath hatred."

"And I presume you are far above it?" she said
very scornfully, and eyed him in silence for a moment.
"You are a poor creature," she pursued, presently. "I
heartily despise you. You suffered yourself to be deceived by a mere trick; you let the woman you loved
go from you without an effort to keep her. You might
have been a queen's lover, and you despised her. And
now, when you could have the woman who did you a
mortal injury be led forth to death before your eyes,
you interceded for her and saved her life. You are
a fool. I despise you."

"I rejoice that you do," returned Zoroaster coldly.
"I would not have your admiration, if I might be paid
for receiving it with the whole world and the wisdom
thereof."

"Not even if you might have for your wife the

woman you loved in your poor, insipid way—but you
loved her nevertheless? She is pale and sorrowful,
poor creature; she haunts the gardens like the shadow
of death; she wearies the king with her wan face.
She is eating her heart out for you—the king took her
from you, you could take her from him to-morrow, if
you pleased. The greater your folly, because you do
not. As for her, her foolishness is such that she would
follow you to the ends of the earth—poor girl! she
little knows what a pale, wretched, sapless thing you
have in your breast for a heart."

But Zoroaster gazed calmly at the queen in quiet
scorn at her scoffing.

"Think you that the sun is obscured, because you
can draw yonder curtain before your window and keep
out his rays?" he asked. "Think you that the children
of light feel pain because the children of darkness say
in their ignorance that there is no light?"

"You speak in parables—having nothing plain to
say," returned the queen, thrusting a golden pin through
her hair at the back and through the folds of her linen
tiara. But she felt Zoroaster's eyes upon her, and
looking up, she was fascinated by the strange light in
them. She strove to look away from him, but could
not. Suddenly her heart sank within her. She had
heard of Indian charmers and of Chaldean necromancers
and wise men, who could perform wonders and slay
their enemies with a glance. She struggled to take
her eyes from his, but it was of no use. The subtle
power of the universal agent had got hold upon her,
and she was riveted to the spot so long as he kept his
eyes upon her. He spoke again, and his voice seemed
to come to her with a deafening metallic force, as
though it vibrated to her very brain.

" You may scoff at me ; shield yourself from me, if you can," said Zoroaster. " Lift one hand, if you are able—make one step from me, if you have the strength. You cannot; you are altogether in my power. If I would, I could kill you as you stand, and there would be no mark of violence upon you, that a man should be able to say you were slain. You boast of your strength and power. See, you follow the motion of my hand, as a dog would. See, you kneel before me, and prostrate yourself in the dust at my feet, at my bidding. Lie there, and think well whether you are able to scoff any more. You kneeled to the king of your own will; you kneel to me at mine, and though you had the strength of a hundred men, you must kneel there till I bid you rise."

The queen was wholly under the influence of the terrible power Zoroaster possessed. She was no more able to resist his will than a drowning man can resist the swift torrent that bears him down to his death. She lay at the priest's feet, helpless and nerveless. He gazed at her for a moment as she crouched before him.

" Rise," he said, " go your way, and remember me."

Relieved from the force of the subtle influence he projected, Atossa sprang to her feet and staggered back a few paces, till she fell upon the couch.

" What manner of man art thou ? " she said, staring wildly before her, as though recovering from some heavy blow that had stunned her.

But she saw Zoroaster's white robes disappear through the door, even while the words were on her lips, and she sank back in stupefaction upon the cushions of the couch.

Meanwhile the trumpets sounded in the courts of

the palace and the guards were marshalled out at the king's command. Messengers mounted and rode furiously up the valley to the fortress, to warn the troops there to make ready for the march; and before the sun reached the meridian, Darius was on horseback, in his armour, at the foot of the great staircase. The blazing noonday light shone upon his polished helmet and on the golden wings that stood out on either side of it, and the hot rays were sent flashing back from his gilded harness, and from the broad scales of his horse's armour.

The slaves of the palace stood in long ranks before the columns of the portico and upon the broad stairs on each side, and Zoroaster stood on the lowest step, attended by a score of his priests, to receive the king's last instructions.

"I go forth, and in two months I will return in triumph," said Darius. "Meanwhile keep thou the government in thy hand, and let not the laws be relaxed because the king is not here. Let the sacrifice be performed daily in the temple, and let all things proceed as though I myself were present. I will not that petty strifes arise because I am away. There shall be peace—peace—peace for ever throughout my kingdom, though I shed much blood to obtain it. And all the people who are evildoers and makers of strife and sedition shall tremble at the name of Darius, the king of kings, and of Zoroaster, the high priest of the All-Wise. In peace I leave you, to cause peace whither I go; and in peace I will come again to you. Farewell, Zoroaster, truest friend and wisest counsellor; in thy keeping I leave all things. Take thou the signet and bear it wisely till I come."

Zoroaster received the royal ring and bowed a low

obeisance.   Then Darius pressed his knees to his horse's sides and the noble steed sprang forward upon the straight, broad road, like an arrow from a bow. The mounted guards grasped their spears and gathered their bridles in their hands and followed swiftly, four and four, shoulder to shoulder, and knee to knee, their bronze cuirasses and polished helmets blazing in the noonday sun and clashing as they galloped on ; and in a moment there was nothing seen of the royal guard but a tossing wave of light far up the valley ; and the white dust, that had risen as they plunged forward, settled slowly in the still, hot air upon the roses and shrubs that hung over the enclosure of the garden at the foot of the broad staircase.

Zoroaster gazed for a moment on the track of the swift warriors ; then went up the steps, followed by his priests, and entered the palace.

Atossa and Nehushta had watched the departure of the king from their upper windows, at the opposite ends of the building, from behind the gilded lattices. Atossa had recovered somewhat from the astonishment and fear that had taken possession of her when she had found herself under Zoroaster's strange influence, and as she saw Darius ride away, while Zoroaster remained standing upon the steps, her courage rose. She resolved that nothing should induce her again to expose herself to the chief priest's unearthly power, and she laughed to herself as she thought that she might yet destroy him, and free herself from him for ever.   She wondered how she could ever have given a thought of love to such a man, and she summoned her black slave, and sent him upon his last errand, by which he was to obtain his freedom.

But Nehushta gazed sadly after the galloping guards,

and her eye strove to distinguish the king's crest before
the others, till all was mingled in the distance, in an
indiscriminate reflection of moving light, and then lost
to view altogether in the rising dust.   Whether she
loved him truly, or loved him not, he had been true
and kind to her, and had rested his dark head upon
her shoulder that very morning before he went, and
had told her that, of all living women, he loved her
best.   But she had felt a quick sting of pain in her
heart, because she knew that she would give her life
to lie for one short hour on Zoroaster's breast and sob
out all her sorrow and die.

CHAPTER XIX.

FOUR days after the king's departure, Nehushta was wandering in the gardens as the sun was going down, according to her daily custom. There was a place she loved well—a spot where the path widened to a circle, round which the roses grew, thick and fragrant with the breath of the coming summer, and soft green shrubs and climbing things that twisted their tender arms about the myrtle trees. The hedge was so high that it cut off all view of the gardens beyond, and only the black north-western hills could just be seen above the mass of shrubbery; beyond the mountains and all over the sky, the glow of the setting sun spread like a rosy veil; and the light tinged the crests of the dark hills and turned the myrtle leaves to a strange colour, and gilded the highest roses to a deep red gold.

The birds were all singing their evening song in loud, happy chorus, as only Eastern birds can sing; the air was warm and still, and the tiny gnats chased each other with lightning quickness in hazy swarms over-head, in the reflected glow.

Nehushta loved the little open space, for it was there that, a year ago, she had sent for Zoroaster to come to her that she might tell him she knew the truth at last. She stood still and listened to the singing of the birds, gazing upwards at the glowing sky, where the red was

fast turning to purple; she breathed in the warm air
and sighed softly; wishing, as she wished every night,
that the sunset might fade to darkness, and there
might be no morning for her any more.

She had lived almost entirely alone since Darius
had gone to Shushan; she avoided Atossa, and she
made no effort to see Zoroaster, who was entirely
absorbed by the management of the affairs of the state.
In the king's absence there were no banquets, as there
used to be when he was in the palace, and the two
queens were free to lead whatever life seemed best to
them, independently of each other and of the courtiers.
Atossa had chosen to shut herself up in the seclusion
of her own apartments, and Nehushta rarely left her
own part of the palace until the evening. But when
the sun was low, she loved to linger among the roses
in the garden, till the bright shield of the moon was
high in the east, or till the faint stars burned in their
full splendour, and the nightingales began to call and
trill their melancholy song from end to end of the
sweet valley.

So she stood on this evening, looking up into the
sky, and her slaves waited her pleasure at a little
distance. But while she gazed, she heard quick steps
along the walk, and the slave-women sprang aside to
let some one pass. Nehushta turned and found herself face to face with Atossa, who stood before her,
wrapped in a dark mantle, a white veil of Indian gauze
wound about her head, and half-concealing her face.
It was a year since they had met in private, and
Nehushta drew herself suddenly to her height, and
the old look of scorn came over her dark features.
She would have asked haughtily what brought Atossa
there, but the fair queen was first in her speech. There

was hardly even the affectation of friendliness in her tones, as she stood there alone and unattended, facing her enemy.

"I came to ask if you wished to go with me," said Atossa.

"Where? Why should I go with you?"

"I am weary of the palace. I think I will go to Shushan to be nearer the king. To-night I will rest at the fortress."

Nehushta stared coldly at the fair woman, muffled in her cloak and veil.

"What is it to me whether you go to the ends of the earth, or whether you remain here?" she asked.

"I wished to know whether you desired to accompany me, else I should not have asked you the question. I feared that you might be lonely here in Stakhar—will you not come?"

"Again I say, why do you ask me? What have I to do with you?" returned Nehushta, drawing her mantle about her as though to leave Atossa.

"If the king were here, he would bid you go," said Atossa, looking intently upon her enemy.

"It is for me to judge what the king would wish me to do—not for you. Leave me in peace. Go your way if you will—it is nothing to me."

"You will not come?" Atossa's voice softened and she smiled serenely. Nehushta turned fiercely upon her.

"No! If you are going—go! I want you not!"

"You are glad I am going, are you not?" asked Atossa, gently.

"I am glad—with a gladness only you can know. I would you were already gone!"

"You rejoice that I leave you alone with your lover. It is very natural——"

"My lover!" cried Nehushta, her wrath rising and blazing in her eyes.

"Ay, your lover! the thin, white-haired priest, that once was Zoroaster—your old lover—your poor old lover!"

Nehushta steadied herself for a moment. She felt as though she must tear this woman in pieces. But she controlled her anger by a great effort, though she was nearly choking as she drew herself up and answered.

"I would that the powers of evil, of whom you are, might strangle the thrice-accursed lie in your false throat!" she said, in low fierce tones, and turned away.

Still Atossa stood there, smiling as ever. Nehushta looked back as she reached the opposite end of the little plot.

"Are you not yet gone? Shall I bid my slaves take you by the throat and force you from me?" But, as she spoke, she looked beyond Atossa, and saw that a body of dark men and women stood in the path. Atossa had not come unprotected.

"I see you are the same foolish woman you ever were," answered the older queen. Just then, a strange sound echoed far off among the hills above, strange and far as the scream of a distant vulture calling its mate to the carrion feast—an unearthly cry that rang high in the air from side to side of the valley, and struck the dark crags and doubled in the echo, and died away in short, faint pulsations of sound upon the startled air.

Nehushta started slightly. It might have been the cry of a wolf, or of some wild beast prowling upon the heights, but she had never heard such a sound before.

But Atossa showed no surprise, and her smile returned to her lips more sweetly than ever—those lips that had kissed three kings, and that had never spoken truly a kind or a merciful word to living man, or child, or woman.

"Farewell, Nehushta," she said, "if you will not come, I will leave you to yourself—and to your lover. I daresay he can protect you from harm.   Heard you that sound ?   It is the cry of your fate.   Farewell, foolish girl, and may every undreamed-of quality of evil attend you to your dying day——"

"Go !" cried Nehushta, turning and pointing to the path with a gesture of terrible anger.   Atossa moved back a little.

"It is no wonder I linger awhile—I thought you were past suffering.   If I had time, I might yet find some way of tormenting you—you are very foolish——"

Nehushta walked rapidly forward upon her, as though to do her some violence with her own hands. But Atossa, as she gave way before the angry Hebrew woman, drew from beneath her mantle the Indian knife she had once taken from her.   Nehushta stopped short, as she saw the bright blade thrust out against her bosom.   But Atossa held it up one moment, and then threw it down upon the grass at her feet.

"Take it !" she cried, and in her voice, that had been so sweet and gentle a moment before, there suddenly rang out a strange defiance and a bitter wrath. "Take what is yours—I loathe it, for it smells of you —and you, and all that is yours, I loathe and hate and scorn !"

She turned with a quick movement and disappeared amongst her slaves, who closed in their ranks behind her, and followed her rapidly down the path.   Nehushta remained standing upon the grass, peering after her retreating enemy through the gloom; for the glow had faded from the western sky while they had been speaking, and it was now dusk.

Suddenly, as she stood, almost transfixed with the horror of her fearful anger, that strange cry rang again through the lofty crags and crests of the mountains, and echoed and died away.

Nehushta's slave-women, who had hung back in fear and trembling during the altercation between the two queens, came forward and gathered about her.

" What is it ?" asked the queen in a low voice, for her own heart beat with the anticipation of a sudden danger.   " It is the cry of your fate," Atossa had said—verily it sounded like the scream of a coming death.

" It is the Druksh of the mountains !" said one.

" It is the howling of wolves," said another, a Median woman from the Zagros mountains.

" The war-cry of the children of Anak is like that," said a little Syrian maid, and her teeth chattered with fear.

As they listened, crouching and pressing about their royal mistress in their terror, they heard below in the road, the sound of horses and men moving quickly past the foot of the gardens.   It was Atossa and her train, hurrying along the highway in the direction of the fortress.

Nehushta suddenly pushed the slaves aside, and fled down the path towards the palace, and the dark women hurried after.   One of them stooped and picked up the Indian knife and hid it in her bosom as she ran.

The whole truth had flashed across Nehushta's mind
in an instant. Some armed force was collecting upon
the hills to descend in a body upon the palace, to
accomplish her destruction. Atossa had fled to a place
of safety, after enjoying the pleasure of tormenting her
doomed enemy to the last moment, well knowing that
no power would induce Nehushta to accompany her.
But one thought filled Nehushta's mind in her instant-
aneous comprehension of the truth; she must find
Zoroaster, and warn him of the danger. They would
have time to fly together, yet. Atossa must have
known how to time her flight, since the plot was hers,
and she had not yet been many minutes upon the
road.

Through the garden she ran, and up the broad steps
to the portico. Slaves were moving about under the
colonnade, leisurely lighting the great torches that
burned there all night. They had not heard the
strange cries from the hills; or, hearing only a faint
echo, had paid no attention to the sound.

Nehushta paused, breathless with running. As she
realised the quiet that reigned in the palace, where the
slaves went about their duties as though nothing had
occurred, or were likely to occur, it seemed to her as
though she must have been dreaming. It was impossible that if there were any real danger, it should not
have become known at least to some one of the
hundreds of slaves who thronged the outer halls and
corridors. Moreover there were numerous scribes and
officers connected with the government; some few
nobles whom Darius had left behind when he went
to Shushan; there were their wives and families resid-
ing in various parts of the palace and in the buildings
below it, and there was a strong detachment of Persian

guards. If there were danger, some one must have known it.

She did not know that at that moment the inhabitants of the lower palace were already alarmed, while some were flying, leaving everything behind, in their haste to reach the fortress higher up the valley. Everything seemed quiet where she was, and she determined to go alone in search of Zoroaster, without raising any alarm. Just as she entered the doorway of the great hall, she heard the cry again echoing behind her through the valley. It was as much as she could do to control the terror that again took hold of her at the dreaded sound, as she passed the files of bowing slaves, and went in between the two tall spearmen who guarded the inner entrance, and grounded their spears with military precision as she went by.

She had one slave whom she trusted more than the rest. It was the little Syrian maid, who was half a Hebrew.

"Go," she said quickly, in her own tongue. "Go in one direction and I will go in another, and search out Zoroaster, the high priest, and bring him to my chamber. I also will search, but if I find him not, I will wait for thee there."

The dark girl turned and ran through the halls, swift as a startled fawn, to fulfil her errand, and Nehushta went another way upon her search. She was ashamed to ask for Zoroaster. The words of her enemy were still ringing in her ears—"alone with your lover;" it might be the common talk of the court for all she knew. She went silently on her way. She knew where Zoroaster dwelt. The curtain of his simple chamber was thrown aside and a faint light burned in the room. It was empty; a scroll lay open upon the floor beside a purple cushion, as he had left it, and his long white mantle lay tossed upon the couch which served him for a bed.

She gazed lovingly for one moment into the open chamber, and then went on through the broad corridor, dimly lighted everywhere with small oil lamps. She looked into the council chamber and it was deserted. The long rows of double seats were empty, and gleamed faintly in the light. High upon the dais at the end, a lamp burned above the carved chair of ivory and gold, whereon the king sat when the council was assembled. There was no one there. Farther on, the low entrance to the treasury was guarded by four spearmen, whose arms clanged upon the floor as the queen passed. But she saw that the massive bolts and the huge square locks upon them were in their places. There was no one within. In the colonnade beyond, a few nobles stood talking carelessly together, waiting for their evening meal to be served them in a brightly illuminated hall, of which the doors stood wide open to admit the cool air of the coming night. The magnificently-arrayed courtiers made a low obeisance and then stood in astonishment as the queen went by. She held up her head and nodded to them, trying to look as though nothing disturbed her.

On and on she went through the whole wing, till she came to her own apartment. Not so much as one white-robed priest had she seen upon all her long search. Zoroaster was certainly not in the portion of the palace through which she had come. Entering her own chambers, she looked round for the little Syrian maid, but she had not returned.

Unable to bear the suspense any longer, she hastily despatched a second slave in search of the chief priest

—a Median woman, who had been with her in Ecbatana.

It seemed as though the minutes were lengthened to hours. Nehushta sat with her hands pressed to her temples, that throbbed as though the fever would burst her brain, and the black fan-girl plied the palm-leaf with all her might, thinking that her mistress suffered from the heat. The other women she dismissed ; and she sat waiting beneath the soft light of the perfumed lamp, the very figure and incarnation of anxiety.

Something within her told her that she was in great and imminent danger, and the calm she had seen in the palace could not allay in her mind the terror of that unearthly cry she had heard three times from the hills. As she thought of it, she shuddered, and the icy fear seemed to run through all her limbs, chilling the marrow in her bones, and freezing her blood suddenly in its mad course.

"Left alone with your lover' —"it is the cry of your fate"—Atossa's words kept ringing in her ears like a knell—the knell of a shameful death ; and as she went over the bitter taunts of her enemy, her chilled pulses beat again more feverishly than before. She could not bear to sit still, but rose and paced the room in intense agitation. Would they never come back, those dallying slave-women ?

The fan-girl tried to follow her mistress, and her small red eyes watched cautiously every one of Nehushta's movements. But the queen waved her off and the slave went and stood beside the chair where she had sat, her fan hanging idly in her hand. At that moment, the Median woman entered the chamber.

"Where is he ?" asked Nehushta, turning suddenly upon her.

The woman made a low obeisance and answered in trembling tones :—

"They say that the high priest left the palace two hours ago, with the queen Atossa. They say——"

"Thou liest!" cried Nehushta vehemently, and her face turned white, as she stamped her foot upon the black marble pavement. The woman sprang back with a cry of terror, and ran towards the door. She had never seen her mistress so angry. But Nehushta called her back.

"Come hither—what else do they say?" she asked, controlling herself as best she could.

"They say that the wild riders of the eastern desert are descending from the hills," answered the slave hurriedly and almost under her breath. "Every one is flying—everything is in confusion—I hear them even now, hurrying to and fro in the courts, the soldiers——"

But, even as she spoke, an echo of distant voices and discordant cries came through the curtains of the door from without, the rapid, uneven tread of people running hither and thither in confusion, the loud voices of startled men and the screams of frightened women—all blending together in a wild roar that grew every moment louder.

Just then, the little Syrian maid came running in, almost tearing the curtains from their brazen rods as she thrust the hangings aside. She came and fell breathless at Nehushta's feet and clasped her knees.

"Fly, fly, beloved mistress," she cried, "the devils of the mountains are upon us—they cover the hills—they are closing every entrance—the people in the lower palace are all slain——"

"Where is Zoroaster?" In the moment of supreme

danger, Nehushta grew calm, and her senses were restored to her again.

"He is in the temple with the priests—by this time he is surely slain—he could know of nothing that is going on—fly, fly!" cried the poor Syrian girl in an agony of terror.

Nehushta laid her hand kindly upon the head of the little maid, and turning in the pride of her courage, now that she knew the worst, she spoke calmly to the other slaves who thronged in from the outer hall, some breathless with fear, others screaming in an agony of acute dread.

"On which side are they coming?" she asked.

"From the hills, from the hills they are descending in thousands," cried half a dozen of the frightened women at once, the rest huddled together like sheep, moaning in their fear.

"Go you all to the farther window," cried Nehushta, in commanding tones. "Leap down upon the balcony —it is scarce a man's height—follow it to the end and past the corner where it joins the main wall of the garden. Run along upon the wall till you find a place where you can descend. Through the gardens you can easily reach the road by the northern gate. Fly and save yourselves in the darkness. You will reach the fortress before dawn if you hasten. You will hasten," she added with something of disdain in her voice, for before she had half uttered her directions, the last of the slave-women, mad with terror, disappeared through the open window, and she could hear them drop, one after the other, in quick succession upon the marble balcony below. She was alone.

But, looking down, she saw at her feet the little Syrian maid, looking with imploring eyes to his face.

"Why do you not go with the rest?" asked Nehushta, stooping down and laying one hand upon the girl's shoulder.

"I have eaten thy bread—shall I leave thee in the hour of death?" asked the little slave, humbly.

"Go, child," replied Nehushta, very kindly. "I have seen thy devotion and truth—thou must not perish."

But the Syrian leaped to her feet, and there was pride in her small face, as she answered:

"I am a bondwoman, but I am a daughter of Israel, even as thou art. Though all the others leave thee, I will not. It may be I can help thee."

"Thou art a brave child," said Nehushta; and she drew the girl to her and pressed her kindly. "I must go to Zoroaster—stay thou here, hide thyself among the curtains—escape by the window, if any come to harm thee." She turned and went rapidly out between the curtains, as calm and as pale as death.

The din in the palace had partially subsided, and new and strange cries re-echoed through the vast halls and corridors. An occasional wild scream—a momentary distant crash as of a door breaking down and thundering upon the marble pavement; and then again, the long, strange cries, mingled with a dull, low sound as of a great moaning—all came up together, and seemed to meet Nehushta as she lifted the curtains and went out.

But the little Syrian maid grasped the Indian knife in her girdle, and stole stealthily upon her mistress's steps.

CHAPTER XX.

NEHUSHTA glided like a ghost along the corridors and dimly-lighted halls. As yet, the confusion seemed to be all in the lower story of the palace, but the roaring din rose louder every moment—the shrieks of wounded women with the moaning of wounded men, the clash of swords and arms, and, occasionally, a quick, loud rattle, as half a dozen arrows that had missed their mark struck the wall together.

Onward she flew, not pausing to listen, lest in a moment more the tide of fight should be forced up the stairs and overtake her. She shuddered as she passed the head of the great staircase and heard, as though but a few steps from her, a wild shriek that died suddenly into a gurgling death hiss.

She passed the treasury, whence the guards had fled, and in a moment more she was above the staircase that led down to the temple behind the palace. There was no one there as yet, as far as she could see in the starlight. The doors were shut, and the massive square building frowned through the gloom, blacker than its own black shadow.

Nehushta paused as she reached the door, and listened. Very faintly through the thick walls she could hear the sound of the evening chant. The priests were all within with Zoroaster, unconscious of their danger and of all that was going on in the palace, singing the hymns of the sacrifice before the sacred fire,—chanting, as it were, a dirge for themselves. Nehushta tried the door. The great bronze gates were locked together, and though she pushed with her whole strength, they would not move a hair's breadth.

"Press the nail nearest the middle," said a small voice behind her. Nehushta started and looked round. It was the little Syrian slave, who had followed her out of the palace, and stood watching her in the dark. Nehushta put her hand upon the round head of the nail and pressed, as the slave told her to do. The door opened, turning slowly and noiselessly upon its hinges. Both women entered; the Syrian girl looked cautiously back and pushed the heavy bronze back to its place. The Egyptian artisan who had made the lock, had told one of the queen's women whom he loved the secret by which it was opened, and the Syrian had heard it repeated and remembered it.

Once inside, Nehushta ran quickly through the corridor between the walls and rushing into the inner temple, found herself behind the screen and in a moment more she stood before all the priests and before Zoroaster himself. But even as she entered, the Syrian slave, who had lingered to close the gates, heard the rushing of many feet outside, and the yelling of hoarse voices, mixed with the clang of arms.

Solemnly the chant rose around the sacred fire that seemed to burn by unearthly means upon the black stone altar. Zoroaster stood before it, his hands lifted in prayer, and his waxen face and snow-white beard illuminated by the dazzling effulgence.

The seventy priests, in even rank, stood around the

walls, their hands raised in like manner as their chief priest's; their voices going up in a rich chorus, strong and tuneful, in the grand plain-chant. But Nehushta broke upon their melody, with a sudden cry, as she rushed before them. ﹒

"Zoroaster—fly—there is yet time. The enemy are come in thousands—they are in the palace. There is barely time!" As she cried to him and to them all, she rushed forward and laid one hand upon his shoulder.

But the high priest turned calmly upon her, his face unmoved, although all the priests ceased their chanting and gathered about their chief in sudden fear. As their voices ceased, a low roar was heard from without, as though the ocean were beating at the gates.   ﹒

Zoroaster gently took Nehushta's hand from his shoulder.

"Go thou, and save thyself," he said kindly. "I will not go. If it be the will of the All-Wise that I perish, I will perish before this altar. Go thou quickly, and save thyself while there is yet time."

But Nehushta took his hand in hers, that trembled with the great emotion, and gazed into his calm eyes as he spoke—her look was very loving and very sad.

"Knowest thou not, Zoroaster, that I would rather die with thee than live with any other? I swear to thee, by the God of my fathers, I will not leave thee." Her soft voice trembled—for she was uttering her own sentence of death.

"There is no more time!" cried the voice of the little Syrian maid, as she came running into the temple. "There is no more time! Ye are all dead men! Behold, they are breaking down the doors!"

As she spoke, the noise of some heavy mass striking

against the bronze gates echoed like thunder through
the temple, and at each blow a chorus of hideous yells
rose, wild and long-drawn-out, as though the fiends of
hell were screaming in joy over the souls of the lost.

The priests drew together, trembling with fear, brave
and devoted though they were. Some of them would
have run towards the door, but the Syrian maid stood
before them.

"Ye are dead men and there is no salvation—ye
must die like men," said the little maid, quietly. "Let
me go to my mistress." And she pushed through the
crowd of white-robed men, who surged together in
their sudden fear, like a white-crested wave heaved up
from the deep by a fierce wind.

Nehushta still held Zoroaster's hand and stared
wildly upon the helpless priests. Her one thought
was to save the man she loved, but she saw well
enough that it was too late. Nevertheless she
appealed to the priests.

"Can none of you save him?" she cried.

Foremost in the little crowd was a stern, dark man
—the same who had been the high priest before
Zoroaster came, the same who had first hurled defiance
at the intruder, and then had given him his whole
allegiance. He spoke out loudly:

"We will save him and thee if we are able," he
cried in brave enthusiasm for his chief. "We will
take you between us and open the doors, and it may
be that we can fight our way out—though we are all
slain, he may be saved." He would have laid hold on
Zoroaster, and there was not one of the priests who
would not have laid down his life in the gallant
attempt. But Zoroaster gently put him back.

"Ye cannot save me, for my hour is come," he said,

and a radiance of unearthly glory stole upon his features, so that he seemed transfigured and changed before them all. "The foe are as a thousand men against one. Here we must die like men, and like priests of the Lord before His altar."

The thundering at the doors continued to echo through the whole temple, almost drowning every other sound as it came; and the yells of the infuriated besiegers rose louder and louder between.

Zoroaster's voice rang out clear and strong and the band of priests gathered more and more closely about him. Nehushta still held his hand tightly between her own, and, pale as death, she looked up to him as he spoke. The little Syrian girl stood beside her mistress, very quiet and grave.

"Hear me, ye priests of the Lord," said Zoroaster. "We are doomed men and must surely die, though we know not by whose hand we perish. Now, therefore, I beseech you to think not of this death which we must suffer in our mortal bodies, but to open your eyes to the things which are not mortal and which perish not eternally. For man is but a frail and changing creature as regards his mortality, seeing that his life is not longer than the lives of other created things, and he is delicate and sickly and exposed to manifold dangers from his birth. But the soul of man dieth not, neither is there any taint of death in it, but it liveth for ever and is made glorious above the stars. For the stars, also, shall have an end, and the earth— even as our bodies must end here this night; but our souls shall see the glory of God, the All-Wise, and shall live.

"The sun riseth and the earth is made glad, and it is day; and again he setteth and it is night, and the whole earth is sorrowful. But though our sun is gone down and we shall see him rise no more, yet shall we see a sun which setteth not for ever, and of whose gladness there is no end. The morning cometh, after which there shall be no evening. The Lord Ahura Mazda, who made all things, made also these our bodies, and put us in them to live and move and have being for a space on earth. And now he demands them again; for he gave them and they are his. Let us give them readily as a sacrifice, for he who knoweth all things, knoweth also why it is meet that we should die. And he who hath created all things which we see and which perish quickly, hath created also the things which we have not seen, but shall see hereafter;—and the time is at hand when our eyes shall be opened to the world which endureth, though they be closed in death upon the things which perish. Raise then a hymn of thanks with me to the All-Wise God, who is pleased to take us from time into eternity, from darkness into light, from change to immortality, from death by death to life undying.

" *Praise we the All-Wise God, who hath made and created the years and the ages;*
Praise him who in the heavens hath sown and hath scattered the seed of the stars;
Praise him who moves between the three ages that are, and that have been, and shall be;
Praise him who rides on death, in whose hand are all power and honour and glory;
Praise him who made what seemeth, the image of living, the shadow of life;
Praise him who made what is, and hath made it eternal for ever and ever,

*Who made the days and nights, and created the dark-
    ness to follow the light,*
*Who made the day of life, that should rise up and
    lighten the shadow of death."*

Zoroaster raised one hand to heaven as he chanted
the hymn, and all the priests sang with him in calm
and holy melody, as though death were not even then
with them.   But Nehushta still held his other hand
fast, and her own were icy cold.

With a crash, as though the elements of the earth
were dissolving into primeval confusion, the great
bronze doors gave way, and fell clanging in—and the
yells of the besiegers came to the ears of the priests,
as though the cover had been taken from the caldron
of hell, suffering the din of the damned and their devils
to burst forth in demoniac discord.

In an instant the temple was filled with a swarm of
hideous men, whose eyes were red with the lust of
blood and their hands with slaughter.   Their crooked
swords gleamed aloft as they pressed forward in the
rush, and their yells rent the very roof.

They had hoped for treasure,—they saw but a handful of white-robed unarmed men, standing around one
taller than the rest; and in the throng they saw two
women.   Their rage knew no bounds, and their screams
rose more piercing than ever, as they surrounded the
doomed band, and overwhelmed them, and dyed their
misshapen blades in the crimson blood that flowed so
red and strong over the fair white vestures.

The priests struggled like brave men to the last.
They grasped their hideous foes by arm and limb and
neck, and tossed some of them back upon their fellows ;
fighting desperately with their bare hands against the

armed murderers. But the foe were a hundred to one, and the priests fell in heaps upon each other while the blood flowed out between the feet of the wild, surging throng, who yelled and slew, and yelled again, as each priest tottered back and fell, with the death-wound in his breast.

At last, one tall wretch, with blood-red eyes and distorted features, leaped across a heap of slain and laid hold of Nehushta by the hair with his reeking hand, and strove to drag her out. But Zoroaster's thin arms went round her like lightning and clasped her to his breast. Then the little Syrian maid raised her Indian knife, with both hands, high above her head, and smote the villain with all her might beneath the fifth rib, that he died in the very act; but ere he had fallen, a sharp blade fell swiftly, like a crooked flash of light, and severed the small hands at the wrist; and the brave, true-hearted little maid fell shrieking to the floor. One shriek—and that was all; for the same sword smote her again as she lay, and so she died.

But Nehushta's head fell forward on the high priest's breast, and her arms clasped him wildly as his clasped her.

"Oh, Zoroaster, my beloved, my beloved! Say not any more that I am unfaithful, for I have been faithful even unto death, and I shall be with you beyond the stars for ever!"

He pressed her closer still, and in that awful moment, his white face blazed with the radiant light of the new life that comes by death alone.

"Beyond the stars and for ever!" he cried. "In the light of the glory of God most high!"

The keen sword flashed out once more and severed

Nehushta's neck, and found its sheath in her lover's heart; and they fell down dead together, and the slaughter was done.

But on the third day, Darius the king returned; for a messenger met him, bringing news that his soldiers had slain the rebels in Ecbatana, though they were ten to one. And when he saw what things had been done in Stakhar, and looked upon the body of the wife he had loved, lying clasped in the arms of his most faithful and beloved servant, he wept most bitterly. And he rode forth and destroyed utterly the wild riders of the eastern hills, and left not one child to weep for its father that was dead. But two thousand of them he brought to Stakhar, and crucified them all upon the roadside, that their blood might avenge the blood of those he had loved so well.

And he took the bodies of Zoroaster the high priest, and of Nehushta the queen, and of the little Syrian maid, and he buried them with spices and fine linen, and in plates of pure gold, together in a tomb over against the palace, hewn in the rock of the mountain.

THE END.